My Life Begins Next Monday...

The 7 Stages of Overcoming Life's Obstacles

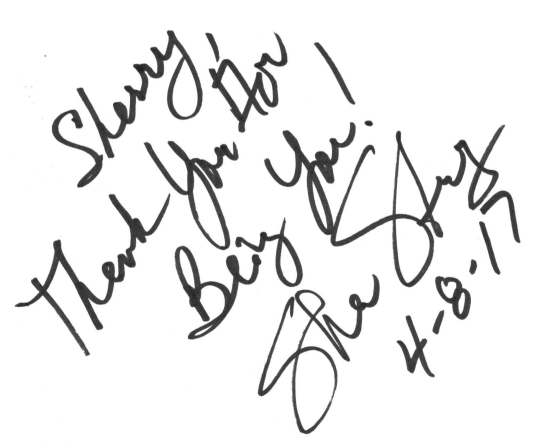

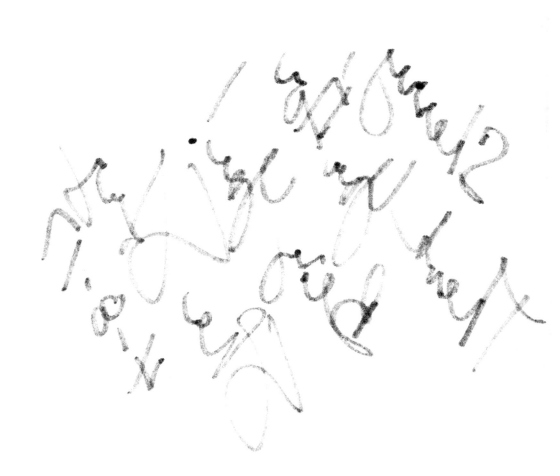

Dedication

Thank you to the friends and family who supported this dream! It was your encouragement that whispered in my ear and kept me going.

Steve Strong- My soul mate!
Jamie Haack- You will find your way.
Ambir Leehy- Always be you; you are awesome!
Josh Schweinfurth- You are such an inspiration! Thank you!
Grandma Huber
Steve and Joan Anderson
Michelle Palermo Harris
Ginny Hicks
Wanda Lyle
Heather and Billy Johnson
Kelly Pratt
Amy Hughes
Jamie Hansen
Dia Matteson
Lisa Te Sla
Melissa Albers
Cheryl Nath (Dear Friend who God has Taken Home)

To my grandchildren--
Tyson, Payten, Kaden, and Isabella.
Always Follow Your Dreams!

Contents:

Dedication..*iii*
Foreword ....*ix*
Introduction... *1*

Chapter 1: Survival..**3**
Chapter 2: Denial..**27**
Chapter 3: Acceptance..**49**
Chapter 4: Motivation **71**
Chapter 5: Confidence..**97**
Chapter 6: Connection **119**
Chapter 7: Grace..**139**

Final Word.. *163*

Foreword

We each have our own unique journey through life. That journey will have many ups and downs, twists and turns. About the only thing predictable about our journeys is that they will be unpredictable much of the time.

What's important is not simply about what actually happens on this journey. It's not about the situations or circumstances we face. Instead, it's about how we respond; it's what we choose to do with what's presented to us that matters most. Learning to choose our responses, to choose where we go from here, is what unlocks what's possible for us.

Personally, a fire ravaged my home when I was just a young kid. I chose, unconsciously, to become shy and withdrawn while also fiercely independent—not wanting to rely on anyone else. This became my story, until many years later. I was on the last train from New Jersey that was cut off from heading into New York on September 11th. I watched the horror unfold from the other side of the Hudson River with thousands of others, knowing many of those thousands were losing loved ones before their eyes. Terrified, filled with heartache, and with tears in my eyes, I knew I had a choice to make, consciously this time. I could remain a victim to what was going on around me, or I could choose to bring more love, connection, and consciousness into the world.

That moment pointed my life in an entirely new direction, kicking off a series of major life choices that, just eight years later, would lead me to become the 32-year old CEO for the Institute for Professional Excellence in Coaching (iPEC), the preeminent accredited coach training organization in the United States with more than 11,000 coaches and leaders trained across 44 countries.

It's this work that allowed me to meet Shari and many other extraordinary individuals who choose to be at the cause of their life, instead of at its effect.

Shari's life journey, with its extraordinary twists and hardships, is one of triumph and happiness. Why? Because of the choices she made, *consciously*.

Shari Strong

Do you see a pattern emerging? I hope so.

These pages are filled with those choices and lessons about how they allow you to overcome life's challenges. Shari helps you navigate 7 stages of overcoming life's obstacles, laying out not just her experiences, but helpful exercises and practices to make your journey just a little smoother, a little happier, and perhaps just a little faster.

No more waiting, the life that is waiting for you begins now.

D. Luke Iorio
President and CEO, Institute for Professional Excellence in Coaching
www.iPECcoaching.com

Introduction

Life has been hard. I've faced a lot of challenges over my lifetime. I had my first baby at 19 and two more by the time I was 21. Two failed marriages. Both ex-husbands had addictions of some kind. I've been broke and spent a night in jail. I've been in a car accident that almost ruined me. I've been dangerously close to ending my own life.

And that's not even the half of it.

But I'm a survivor. And while the person I am today doesn't much resemble the girl I was so many decades ago, her story helped shape me. It's a part of me and always will be. God has used my struggles to prepare me for the purpose he had in mind for my life all along.

And part of that purpose is sharing my story in a way that powerfully impacts those who hear it.

This book has been swirling in my head and heart since I was 21 years old. I had the title in mind and everything. In fact, this book was the one hope I clung to for many days, weeks, months, and years of struggle. I used it to get myself through so many hard things. At the other end of a dark tunnel, I could see that book up ahead, calling my name.

But I wasn't ready to write it yet. I tried a few years ago, but the words I wrote left me feeling depressed when I read them. Not quite the effect I was going for.

Looking back, I realize I couldn't write my book because my story wasn't finished (it still isn't!). Specifically, I hadn't made it through all seven stages of overcoming life's obstacles: Survival, Denial, Acceptance, Motivation, Confidence, Connection, Grace.

Now I have. And my story is ready to be shared with the world.

Am I saying you have to experience all seven before you live your purpose or dream? No. Not at all! You can be encouraged in knowing we all struggle with finding our purpose. Whether it's our purpose in our jobs, our relationships, or a small project.

Here is what I can tell you: "I'm not there yet either, friends, but I know where I'm going, and you can too."

Knowing your destination makes all the difference. And that's what I hope to show you in this book. I want to give you a goal, an end point. And when you do reach "the end" (which, pardon the cliché, is really just the beginning), your life will have more meaning; your career will have direction; and you will make a greater impact on the people you meet.

Your life has a purpose. That's a fact. Maybe your story is not as dramatic as mine (or maybe it's much more so!), but it's all yours. And God has a plan for that story even now. So many people, who have known me for years, have told me, "Shari, you've always known what you were going to do. I just don't have that."

Just because you don't know your purpose doesn't mean you don't have one. My hope is to help you identify it, own it, and share it with others.

If that scares you to death, never fear! I'm going to walk you through each step of the way by sharing my own story to inspire you. We'll do this together. We'll move from Survival to Denial to Acceptance to Motivation to Confidence to Connection to Grace, and we'll be better people for the journey.

Come along with me as we find purpose in our pain and blessings in our trials. We'll learn how to own our struggles and use them to influence those in our circles, no matter how big or small. And we'll find out why having a clear understanding of who we are is key to a fulfilled life.

There's no time like right now to get started, friend! We don't have a minute to waste!

Shari

Author's Note: Some of the names and locations have been changed to protect the best interests of those involved.

Chapter 1: Survival

Sometimes even to live is an act of courage.

-Seneca

1

He slammed me up against the cement wall, his hands around my throat. I was seven months pregnant and completely helpless against him. He lifted me up so my tiptoes were barely touching the floor. I held on to his wrists with my fingertips and struggled to breathe.

"I'm going to die," I thought to myself. "I'm going to take my last breath right here in this basement."

Today Is All There Is
I made it through that harrowing experience (obviously), but so much of my young adult life was nothing more than day-to-day (if not minute-to-minute) survival.

"I've just got to get through this day," I'd think to myself. "If I can just get through this day."

That's what Survival is all about. Today. This minute. It's impossible to spend time thinking about tomorrow when you don't even know if you'll still be around for it.

Survival: endurance under adverse or unusual circumstances. We've all been there, and the Survival stage is a tough place to be. A person living in the Survival Stage doesn't have the time or energy to dream; it takes everything he or she has just to make it through the next five minutes, the next hour, the rest of the night.

And then it starts all over again in the morning.

It's frustrating. And exhausting. And crushing. A person living in the Survival Stage loses all hope. Dreams fade away. Nothing matters but the very next step in front of you. The life is sucked out of you more and more every single day. You become nothing more than a shadow of the brilliant, beautiful person you were created to be.

Can you relate to this exhausting kind of life?

When you're here, there's no big picture, just the next step directly in front of you. If you're unable to dream right now, if you can't even think of anything you want out of life, you're in Survival Mode. It is the ultimate feeling of "stuck." How can you dream five years into the future when you have no idea if you'll make it to tomorrow?

Survival Mode doesn't even give us the chance to beat ourselves up. We are just living in the moment with no idea, direction, or purpose other than living right now.

Throughout this book, I am going to ask you to reflect. This isn't a book to just read and forget about. I want you to be aware of your thoughts throughout each chapter. This book is about YOU.

Living a Nightmare
Most days in Survival Mode are just plain hard. Some are really, really hard. Some are nightmarish. I've had my share of all of them.

I briefly described one of the more awful incidents at the beginning of this chapter. I was pregnant with my first child, a daughter. My husband Richard and I (and my two young step-sons) had just moved into our own house in Sioux City, Iowa. It was a cute house and, on good days, it really felt like home. Richard had gotten laid off from his job and had crossed the picket line because we needed an income so badly. We recognized the union's beliefs about solidarity and effecting change, but we needed to eat.

His union co-workers were ticked at his betrayal and sought revenge. They were unscrupulous. They threw a brick through our car front window and slashed our tires. It was our only vehicle. They went as far as hanging our dog from a tree limb in our front yard. People can be so cruel, and it was awful. We spent long nights taking turns staying awake out of fear that our home (or worse, our family) would be hurt.

I vividly remember the day I said, "I am done." I couldn't take it anymore. Richard was at the end of his rope, too. For him, that meant falling back into self-destructive behaviors like smoking pot and dealing drugs. When he was in a stressful situation, he careened out of control. This lack of self-control manifested itself in angry outbursts. When I told him I was done, he took that to mean I was done with him too. One night, the reality of the situation finally hit home and he got so angry he grabbed me by the hair and pulled me through the kitchen. I tried to stay on my feet while he dragged me down the old wooden stairs into the cold, damp, cinder block basement.

He shoved me up against the nearest empty wall, hands gripped around my neck, and lifted me up in the air, choking me. To this day,

My Life Begins Next Monday...

I can remember the old washer and dryer running, shaking loudly, beside me.

With the tips of my toes barely touching the floor, and his hands around my neck, my fingers gripped his wrists as I kept my chin tilted up just enough to breathe. My first thought was, "I can't leave Kip and Ben." My second thought: "This is it. I'm going to die."

> *My second thought: "This is it. I'm going to die."*

We don't know what we're capable of surviving until we're backed in a corner. This time, for me, it was literal.

We had no money. Richard couldn't hold down a job and spent most of his time smoking pot and getting high. He couldn't control how we were living; he couldn't control his future at his job; and it all led to him being out of control. We were just surviving. And barely at that.

When we did have food, it was almost always ham and beans. Cheap, easy, and we could make a big pot of it and eat it day after day after day until it was gone. At one point, Richard worked at Long John Silver's. It was a job with benefits. By benefits, I mean, one of the perks was bringing home leftover fish and chicken each night. This was a treat… at first.

For four months, we ate nothing but beans, ham, fried fish, and chicken—heavy, greasy, unhealthy food. We weren't smart enough to sign up for food stamps or even go to a food pantry. We didn't know what we didn't know.

The Nightmare Continues

The tension in our home hit an all-time high when the pipes in our backyard burst, and it smelled like an old bathroom that had never been cleaned. With all the diapers I had changed, that smell is something you don't forget. We needed to call our landlord but couldn't, because we were a few months behind on our rent.

Whenever Richard would realize he couldn't take care of us, his anger would take over, and shit would hit the fan. This was one of those times, and we were all on guard. Take Richard's stress and our dire circumstances, add in my immaturity and all the heavy, unhealthy food we'd been eating, and it was a recipe for disaster.

It was Richard's beautiful little boys, Kip (2) and Ben (3), who were most often the objects of Richard's wrath.

One day in particular will be engrained in my soul forever. The boys had grown up in this atmosphere and were always nervous and noticeably scared when their dad was around. The interesting thing? I still remember how much they loved him. I remember how they would look at Richard with their big blue eyes, just wanting to be loved by him, to have his approval, even at the ages of two and three.

That particular night the boys were sitting at the kitchen table eating ham and beans. Richard's anger upset Ben so much he threw up. Beans and ham flowed out of his mouth, with the gagging sounds to match, onto his plate. This caused a chain reaction. Kip started heaving and threw up next, and I followed suit.

"Richard, you've got to stop!" I yelled at him. "They are scared! You're making them sick! This has to stop!"

My words did nothing but make his rage worse. He stormed over to the boys, grabbed them by the back of their heads like he was grabbing a football, and he pushed their faces in the fresh vomit. Their noses were buried. It was like a trainer who makes a dog eat its own feces to get it to stop pooping in the yard. If they wouldn't eat the vomit fast enough, Richard would feed it to them. They'd eat, throw up, eat, throw up, and would never cry. It's like they were institutionalized.

Then, if that wasn't horrific and insane enough, as punishment for not being able to keep the regurgitated food down, he stood them in the corner. They were instructed to put their hands in the air above their head, and he made them stand on their tiptoes. If their heels touched the ground, he'd slap their calves with a flip-flop or shoe. They would stand in the corner for two or three hours. Their little legs shook, and they softly wept, asking to go to their room.

That was one of the worst days of my life. It was hard enough to live like this myself. It was another level of awful to watch it happen to two innocent little boys I loved so much.

You may be asking yourself, why didn't she do something? It's not that I didn't want to. It's not that I didn't know right from wrong. But, if he was willing to do this to his two biological children, what do you think my punishment would be if I tried to step in? I was pregnant with our second child during this time. Our oldest was a few months old. What if she started crying? What would he do to her? Not only was I just surviving, the lives of these three little people were at risk too. We never know how we will act or react in any situation, especially if we are living in the Survival Stage.

> *When you are in the Survival Stage, living isn't a long-term verb.*

When you are in the Survival Stage, living isn't a long-term verb. As you begin to own your story or begin to understand someone close to you (your employees or people in your community), please resist the temptation to judge. Moving forward is something every person in this stage wants to do, but it's not as simple or as easy as it sounds. Most likely, they just don't know how to get out.

It's the same when someone is feeling less-than in their job, a relationship, or anything else they are trying to survive.

There's Always a Flicker of Hope
I share these things to put the rest of this book, the rest of my story, into perspective. No matter what you've been through, what you're going through, there is more to life than just surviving. At times, my life was hard, but, in the midst of the hardest times, there was a flicker of hope. I couldn't always see it, but it was there.

I now know that, when I have those moments where I am ready

to give up on myself or a situation, I stop and take a breath. I rely on my understanding that with great struggle comes great reward. It's the learning that gives us hope. At the end of each chapter, I am going to ask you to reflect and ask yourself questions. My goal is not just to share a few stories; it is to help you lead yourself and/or others to a more fulfilled life and career.

By the grace of God, today, Richard is living with his son, Ben. Ben provides a roof for him and gives him the love Richard couldn't show him many years ago. Ben turned out to be a wonderful, caring, amazing family man who has four children of his own. He's loving and caring for his father who was so cruel to him when he was little. It's a miracle really. And a testimony to the hope that lies dormant in all of our Survival stories.

We are never too far gone to hope. It's not about how big or small a thing you overcame. It's about the reality that you overcame it.

What's Your Story?
Identifying our story (or stories) is where we start to discover our real purpose. We all have a Survival story. A time in our lives when something was hard, something went wrong, when things seemed to be falling apart all around us—and we made it through.

In our society, we tend to celebrate the extreme stories—the man who cut off his arm to survive a boulder falling on him, the skiers who found their way out of a blizzard, the woman who escaped after being abducted and tortured. Because of these extreme examples, we tend to not recognize our own stories.

When you stack your story up against some of those larger-than-life doozies, it can seem pretty insignificant.

It's not.

Your story, your life, is packed with meaning. And it's unique to you. That's the best part about it. No one else has lived your exact story, with your exact characters and setting and plot details. Your story may have similarities to someone else's, but it's still one-of-a-kind.

I eventually lived in a home for abused women for about three months. While there, we were required to attend recovery meetings, speak with a psychologist, and partake in daily duties to earn our stay.

I'll never forget one young lady who was so quiet. She didn't speak for the first few weeks. Eventually, she started to tell her story. As she opened her hand, which was always closed in a tight fist, she revealed the bullet her ex-husband had given her and told her it was the bullet he was going to kill her with. She had to carry it with her everywhere she went. If she left it on her dresser, in the bathroom, in the kitchen, and he found it, that would be her last day alive.

Can you imagine?

I had taught myself to always put on a smiling face and "stay positive." So, in my mind, since I was positive, my past wasn't as bad as hers. Maybe it was, maybe it wasn't. I just wasn't ready to own my situation, my story.

One of the things I have learned and want to share with you is this: do not compare yourself. Don't compare how you handle situations with the way your team handles situations. Don't compare your education (or lack thereof) with someone else's. Don't compare or measure where you are in life. All of our challenges weave together as part of our larger purpose.

You Are Right Where You Are Supposed To Be.

Tomorrow you will be too. So, in light of that, what *can* you do today?

You Are Right Where You Are Supposed To Be.

Own It

We need to identify and own our stories and decisions so we can learn from them. Once we've learned from them, we can share them with others. This is so vital when we get to the Connection Stage. Our stories become so powerful when we identify, own, learn from, and share them.

Sometimes owning our Survival stories can be tough. We may be feeling shame, disappointment, bitterness, or a myriad of other emotions that keep us from accepting them as our own. We'd often rather push them down and forget they ever happened.

But that won't do anyone any good.

When my children used to complain about things in their past or tried to blame me for things that were hard, I would encourage them to accept the past as part of their stories.

Yes, I made mistakes as a parent. No, I didn't always make the right decisions while I was trying to survive. Yes, as teenagers they lost their large house on a lake and all their cool toys after a divorce and a terrible car accident (more on that later).

But they survived.

And instead of being resentful or angry (or any other negative emotion), they can be proud of that fact. They can own their Survival stories and choose to make them into something positive.

I want to point out, though, that owning what you have overcome does not mean you get to be a martyr. When we develop a martyr complex, we tend to feel entitled. There is a big difference between owning and acting like a martyr.

If you have had to survive (either one specific event or throughout your lifetime), own it! Don't be ashamed of bad decisions. Learn from them. Don't resent how others treated you; let it go and use it for good. It's important, at this point, to make clear that you should not expect others to pat you on the back for surviving anything. This is all about *you* learning about *you*, and what *you* are meant to do moving forward (and hopefully helping others). This is not about telling your story for others to feel sorry for you.

Start thinking about the specific parts of your life that are hard for you to own. Why do you think that is? (If you are reading this for your job, then: What is something specific with your work situation that is hard for you to own or admit?)

On the flip side, we should also reflect on parts of our lives we can be proud of. Those aspects might be harder to think of, but they're there. What are some things in your life or career you can take pride in and be thankful for?

Your Story is for Learning
The third part, the part that makes everything worthwhile, is this: learn from your story. It's important. So important. There really is nothing

more powerful on earth than someone learning from overcoming a struggle. This leads to influencing others, which leads to purpose. When you learn from your own experiences, your ability to connect with others goes up, way up. Have you ever met someone who had all the answers and never admitted their mistakes or what they have learned? Were they able to connect with you? Did you *want* to connect with them?

Whether you believe this or not, when we show we are not perfect (and are comfortable enough to share it), someone is waiting with bated breath to learn from us. Maybe it's just one person. Maybe it's a small circle of friends. Maybe it's a large group of people.

Maybe it's millions of people all around the world.

One thing I have learned is that those who journal, write books, or even movies, are who we look to for advice. So, even if you never have plans to share your story in a structured fashion, if you plan on working with people at all, your ability to connect with them will rely on you knowing and understanding yourself.

So, if we typically look to those who write down their thoughts, how can you learn from yourself?

Write your thoughts down.

You can start right now. If you haven't even processed in your own mind and heart the importance of "why" you are alive (which could be one reason you are reading this book), then trust the history of the world and start writing.

Write out why you feel you have had to live in the Survival Stage in the past. What purpose do you think it served in the overall scheme of your life? Who are some people you might touch or influence with your story in the future?

The Survival Stage does serve a purpose.

The Survival Stage does serve a purpose. When we're in it, we move forward. We don't get hurt by outside things. When faced with obstacles, we just move around them. We may not overcome them, but we're able to set them aside. We may not have a large world perspective when living in Survival, but our perspective develops a foundation for our future opinions and ideological beliefs.

To develop our identity, sometimes we have to develop our self-governing rules and values. The Survival Stage allows us to learn, day-by-day, how to establish our convictions.

We have choices. For many, if they were not taught how to make choices growing up, were abused, held back for any reason, or rejected (overtly or covertly), the Survival Stage helps them learn how to make decisions and develops their adult identity.

Back in Survival Land
I want to take a minute to share a word of caution with you. Unfortunately, we don't always get a one-way ticket out of the Survival Stage. Sometimes we work our tails off to get out, only to find ourselves right back in it a few days, weeks, or months later.

I rode a roller coaster once (the Boomerang) against my better judgment. I was pretty sure it would make me sick based on the fact that I had always gotten sick in the past. Yet, I did it. Things started out okay.

We don't always get a one-way ticket out...

Surprisingly, I survived the two crazy loops and the twist that went upside down. I congratulated myself when the ride stopped and I hadn't thrown up, passed out, or died. My smug smile froze on my face when the ride started moving again. Backwards! And that part of the story didn't end well. Let's just say, for the rest of the day, I was known as the woman who lost her lunch and shut down the Boomerang.

Isn't life like that sometimes? We get through something really hard, we congratulate ourselves, and then, before we can even catch our breath, the Ride of Life starts going again, except backward. With new twists and turns. And we lose our cookies all over the place.

We end up back in the Survival Stage.

The good news is: each time we find ourselves "just surviving," it gets easier and easier for us to get out and move forward. And eventually to stay out. Life will hit you hard again, sometime in your lifetime, but you'll have the necessary skills to get back on your feet and on with your life.

Surviving Something New
Often, you'll find yourself in the Survival Stage because you've taken a leap of faith into something scary and brand-new. Something that will ultimately be for your good and be an amazing blessing in your life, but at first, it's just hard and frightening.

When I left my successful corporate job and struck out on my own, that whole first year, it didn't take long to fall back into the Survival Stage. I was operating day-to-day out of fear (mostly fear that I would fail).

I would tell myself, "If you can just survive today…" I didn't even let myself think about vacations or even going out to dinner. I felt like I hadn't earned it. When you're in the mode of surviving something, it's hard to come at things from a place of abundance.

I just wanted to survive the year. I had given myself a goal. In order to justify leaving a six-figure income, I gave myself a year to get on my feet. I was tricking myself into moving forward, to not give up until I'd stuck it out for 365 days. I wasn't going to make any decisions until I'd survived the year.

Even with all the trials of my past, it was one of the hardest years of my life.

Every day, during the first six months, I cried, "Oh, my God. I'm spending my *entire* 401K, everything I've saved for/built up for 25 years. I gave it all up. What have I done?"

Often, I find business owners giving up, because they forgot or didn't know the mindset they would need. One of the single most important things you need as a new (and veteran) business owner, as a new mother, or new anything, is perseverance, stick-to-it-ive-ness.

Perseverance can't be taught. It has to be lived.

Perseverance can't be taught. It has to be lived. There's no way someone can teach someone else how to persevere. It's something you have to find for yourself. You have to push yourself through something hard, stick with it no matter what, no matter how badly you want to quit. Trials and tribulations teach perseverance.

That was me my first year as a business owner.

I can't hand you the gift of perseverance. You have to earn it. You're going to have to go through something, survive something, and not give up. When you fail, you're going to have to try again. This is how we earn the ability to persevere.

When you dig in your heels, ride it out, refuse to give up, that's when you know you're where you're supposed to be. That is when you're living your purpose or learning how.

You are moving in the right direction, friend. Take a deep breath, and keep going.

I am going to say this again, as you begin to own your story or begin to understand someone close to you (your employees or people in your community), please resist the temptation to judge. Learning to move forward, reflecting on decisions we have made and how those decisions affected those around us, is an important step. It's not about living in the past and trying to "fix" it. This is about reflecting so we can move forward.

I had a friend tell me, "We don't drive looking in the rearview mirror. But we need to glance back every once in a while, and then we keep going forward."

It's Your Turn!
I'm so excited for you to take what you've read in this chapter and apply it to your own personal life and career. It's going to take some time and

effort (go to www.MyLifeBeginsNextMonday.com and download the free personal e-journal with all the chapter applications), but you have my money-back guarantee it will be worth every second.

The following is a guide in the form of questions to raise your awareness of the Survival Stage. If you truly want to lead yourself to a higher level of awareness, or you want to help or lead others, reflecting on your own experiences will build your ability to spot when someone is living in the Survival Stage. And understanding your own story will lead you to a higher level of living as you help and lead others to achieve their greatest potential.

Take this part of the book seriously, and be intentional in your growth.

Are you ready??

THE APPLICATION BLUEPRINT

It's one thing to read about my life experiences in Survival Stage, but like I said at the beginning of the book, this thing is ultimately about YOU.

1. Take a moment and think about your lowest point (both in your personal life and in your career), times when you truly thought, "I don't know if I'm going to survive this."

It doesn't have to be dramatic as my basement story. It may have been with your parents, financially, or a situation with a friend that hurt your heart. All of our stories are important and define who we are.

Now write those stories down. Include the year, the situation, and why it was your lowest point.

Personal: _____
_____
_____
_____
_____

Career: _____
_____
_____
_____
_____

2. What are some intense emotions you felt during that time? How were others in your life affected? How did it make you feel?

Write those emotions down. Be honest. Hiding your true feelings won't help anyone.

I felt: _____
_____
_____
_____
_____

The other people in my life that were affected: _____
_____
_____
_____
_____
_____

How did I feel about those people? _____
_____
_____
_____
_____
_____

3. Now ask yourself: "What did I learn?"

The answer will give you direction for your next step.

Personal Situation:

I learned: _____
_____
_____
_____
_____

Now, I want to: _____
_____
_____
_____
_____

Career Situation:

I learned: _____
_____
_____
_____
_____

Now, I want to _____
_____
_____
_____
_____

4. If you've made it through the Survival Stage, looking back, what do you think the purpose of those obstacles were?

Don't be shy. Write them down. If you haven't seen any miracles yet, your time will come.

Personal: _____
_____
_____
_____
_____

Career: _____
_____
_____
_____
_____

This is a great start, friend! You should be proud of yourself. The next stage—Denial—is another difficult one to talk about and reflect on but, if you persevere, if you don't give up, we'll get to the exciting stages soon.

It's so important that you not skip any of these steps. Working through these stages, one by one, will help you heal and deal and move forward into all you can be.

THE TAKEAWAY

What is one thing you can take away from this chapter and apply to your personal life?

_____
_____
_____

What is one thing you can take away from this chapter and apply to your business or career?

_____
_____
_____

What is one tangible, practical thing you can do today that will make a difference tomorrow?

_____
_____
_____

My Life Begins Next Monday...

The Circles Outside the Box

They say the world is round
And I am supposed to believe.
Yet this box my heart sits in
Knows this cannot be the only way to exist.
Its sharp edges and black and white shadows
Yearn for rounded rainbows and shades of grey.

This box leaves no room for extra pieces
As it has to shut neatly and close when you are ready.
My heart is at the bottom and it didn't
Know it had a choice.
Please don't surround it with meaningless bits
You don't need.

This box I live in is a sad
Place to be.
It took time to see the cracks in the tape and
Have the courage to let you know.
The actual value you put with this box
Isn't within it, but outside where the circles are merging

Chapter 2: Denial

The greatest barrier to someone achieving their potential is their denial of it.

–Simon Travaglia

2

For so long, every single Wednesday, I would take one of my few dollars and buy a lottery ticket. And I had convinced myself I was going to win. I'd go so far as to write down the exact number of the jackpot for that week and start subtracting my bills one by one.

One million, one hundred thousand, two hundred sixty-two dollars… minus… one hundred twenty-one dollars (electric bill) …minus…seven hundred dollars for groceries… minus…forty-two dollars (water bill) and so on. I was in Denial of my whole situation. Imagining the lottery was going to save me from my dire circumstances. Instead of facing what was in front of me and figuring out some realistic ways to improve my life, I dreamed of winning the lottery and being rescued from it all in one fell swoop.

Denial is the toughest stage to live in.

Denial is the toughest stage to live in. Our spirits are inherently meant for a joyful, peaceful existence. When that isn't happening, our state of mind can transport us into a different world so we can cope. Often that manifests in our physical being, turning to alcohol, depression, living in a dream world or, sadly, acting out in violence or self-destruction.

Dreaming is one of the reasons I am still on this earth. My dreams got me through so many rough days. But I confused my dreams with goals. I was living in a fantasy world and could not accept the reality of my real world. I often had the mindset that, if I just wished hard enough, prayed hard enough, good things would happen to me, and my dreams would come true. I believed something or someone would come to me. I didn't understand that it begins with me. I didn't have the know-how to start making the changes in my life that would help me achieve my goals.

Now I do.

While you read on, my question is: have you ever been in Denial of a situation, a relationship, or maybe the potential at your current job, and imagined unrealistic dreams to get you through?

Living Life in Denial
A person in Denial does one of two things: blames someone else for his or her circumstances or refuses to accept that those circumstances are really happening. If you are unwilling to accept the truth or your circumstances, you're in Denial.

Denial is a necessary coping mechanism. When things are so bad we just can't accept them, or admit them, complete and total Denial helps us keep going in spite of that. Then, when we are able, we can deal with the truth of our life. Denial allows us to cope with things until the time we're physically, emotionally, or mentally ready to handle them.

Unfortunately, the downfall of this mechanism is many of us just stay in the Denial Stage because we're afraid to move to the next stage. Or maybe we conjure up enough courage to move on, but then it's too hard, and we're right back in the World of Denial.

Can you think of a time when you were in Denial about your circumstances? (If you are having trouble thinking of one single time, and are not happy with something in your life or career, you're likely in Denial right now.)

The World of "If"
When you're living in Survival and Denial, you live on ifs. If *this* happens, we'll be able to make our payment. If *that* happens, we'll be able to go to Wal-Mart and get groceries. The ifs are what keep you going.

Early in my first marriage, Richard and I needed a car, so we went to the Buy Here Pay Here car lot (they were very big in the 90's). We were set up to pay bi-weekly. Who were we kidding? We didn't have the money to make the payments. We bought a car on a big if (just like many who purchase automobiles from these fine establishments).

It's not just individuals though. Entrepreneurs, executives, people leading teams around the world predict and forecast on ifs. *If* this happens, and *if* that happens, we will do this or accomplish that. *If* our community does this, *if* our city grows, *if* we stop sending troops to other countries. If you don't have data to back up your decisions or predictions, it is no different than when Richard and I bought a car from Buy Here Pay Here.

In our case, our *ifs* didn't come to fruition. Our income didn't increase, and we couldn't magically pay our expensive car bill. One morning, Richard walked out of the apartment to go to work, and when he got to our assigned parking spot, his heart sank. Our car was gone. We immediately assumed it had been stolen. We didn't know how the repossession industry worked—that they secretly scope you out to reclaim their property with the least amount of resistance and confrontation. Our ignorance paid off for them. Our car had been repossessed overnight.

Knowing you have no other options or answers than what lies at the other end of the *if* can be enough to shut you down completely. So, in a way, *ifs* keep you going. Given our emotional maturity levels, if we would have known when our car was going to be taken back, worse things could have happened. Unrealistic dreams are okay for a small amount of time, just to keep you going one more day.

Eventually, those ifs just may nudge you into a place where you can leave the worlds of Survival and Denial and move into the third stage: Acceptance.

Baby Steps Out of Denial
Losing the car was the next-to-last straw. We didn't have much left at this point—just a small TV on a milk crate in the living room, a card table and four chairs for dining, and a bed for each of the boys. And our one prized possession: a king-sized waterbed. It was one of those with the big blue bladder in it and a headboard made of woven wool. It was very modern at the time and *so* cool.

The boys and I were doing laundry one day. We always folded the clothes on our big waterbed. I would fold, and the boys would place the clothes and towels in the proper pile. To this day, it's the daily chores that make me feel normal when I am having anxiety about other things in life that feel out of control.

Halfway through our task, for a split second, I heard a faint cracking sound. Then, in the next second, a bomb went off! Or so I thought. In the next second, the frame of the bed was on the floor and the boys were tossed onto the floor.

The 200-gallon bladder collapsed! Water was flowing like a flood in the plains after a bad drought. I grabbed the boys and ran out of the apartment. We didn't have a phone, so we had to go to the neighbors' and call my parents who lived across town at that time. I took the boys outside to wait. Looking up at the third floor of our apartment building, there was water rushing out of the walls and down the side of the building.

It seems so surreal now. We had almost nothing before; now we really had nothing! That evening my dad brought his water vacuum over, and we sucked up water for hours. The next day my mother sat down, and we had one of our first real talks that I remember. She asked me if this is how I wanted to live the rest of my life. I honestly don't remember how that conversation transitioned to me telling Richard it was over. But, the next thing I knew, Richard and the boys were standing at the bus depot waiting to go back to Texas.

I moved in with my parents. I applied for a few jobs, but I had no self-esteem and no idea how to cope with anything. Now I was pregnant, my mom and I didn't get along, and my maturity level hadn't changed. That arrangement lasted about six weeks.

Not knowing what else to do, I denied the fact that Richard and I were both clueless, and, together, we were two people who had no real idea about the responsibility adult life would require. I packed my bags and drove pregnant back to Texas, right back into my life of Survival and Denial. Finally, something I knew how to do. It wasn't long until we were eating ham and beans again.

And nothing had changed. Richard was smoking and selling drugs again. We were able to move into apartments or small homes on very little, then never pay the rent. This is how, looking back, sales became a career path. My ability to talk landlords into letting us move in without a deposit, was a talent. We would lose one place and go to another. Eventually, though, our luck ran out.

My Life Begins Next Monday...

We moved in with Richard's parents. I remember some days just lying on the bed and talking to my nine-month-old. "As soon as I have this baby, we're going to leave. We're going to have a better life." I would take myself and my two kids and... well... my life would begin next Monday. OUR lives would begin next Monday.

...my life would begin next Monday.

This was me dreaming. *If* I can just do this... *then* I can do this. My dreams might have been unrealistic, but at least I was daring to imagine a better life for myself. I just didn't know how to actually make it happen. And I never really believed I deserved it.

The only income I had was the loose change I stole from my father-in-law's dresser. Every day, I would go into his room and steal quarters, dimes, nickels, and pennies, knowing I would need it if I were going to leave someday. At this point, though, I couldn't call my parents. I had too much pride, and we weren't on the best of terms. Over time, all those coins I kept secretly accumulating, in a shoe box, added up to just over $100. I went out and bought the best car a hundred bucks could buy (which wasn't much). My new ride was a great big blue boat of a car. The doors opened with a screwdriver; the trunk opened with a screwdriver; and the key holder was missing, so the car started with a screwdriver.

I attempted to leave multiple times and always ended up coming back. The time I finally had the courage to leave for good, Richard, Kip, and Ben stood watching me and their baby sisters loading into that car. Waving their little hands. It was one of the hardest things I have ever done. I wanted to bring them with me, but I hadn't officially adopted them, so they weren't mine to take.

I had to make an excruciating choice: raise four kids in abominable conditions, or get out and leave two behind. At the age of 19, I had to pick which two kids I would save. Just writing about it puts a knot in my stomach, and the guilt pierces my heart.

I don't think Richard believed I would be gone for long, Every time I left for a better life I always came back. I knew he loved me as much as he was able, but he just couldn't take care of all of us. That day, when I left, I never looked back.

After our apartment flooded, people had given us furniture that we had placed it in a storage unit once we moved in with my in-laws. The day I left, I went to that storage unit with some rope, dragged a small dresser and a chair out, loaded up the trunk, and tied as much as I could to the top of the car. I knew I'd need money for formula (Ambir was 3 months old, Jamie was 14 months old), and selling this furniture was the best (and only) plan I had. Then we headed north to Omaha.

I stopped in Oklahoma City and pawned off everything to get a few dollars for formula and gas. I had no driver's license, no insurance, no license plate, nothing (a recurring theme in my life). In those days, it took 15 hours to drive from Texas to Nebraska, because the speed limit was 55. I drove all night with just a couple stops for diaper changes and bottles.

We got all the way to the edge of Omaha. We were at the Offutt Air force Base exit. I remember the sun had just risen, and it was so bright. It was around 7:00 a.m. and, when I took a quick glance in the rear view mirror, it wasn't the sun shining; it was lights flashing. Yes, I was getting pulled over.

As the officer approached my car, all I could think was, "Really? I made it this far, I'm so tired, and now I am getting pulled over?"

He asked for all the information one should have: title, license, insurance, but I didn't have any of that. I showed him my empty wallet, my babies lying on the front seat, and I had no energy to argue or make excuses. He asked me a few questions, and eventually, he asked where I was headed. With a tone of hopelessness, I answered him, and he proceeded to escort me to my parents' home. To this day, I'm thankful for the mercy I was shown by that officer.

I didn't realize it at the time, but I was moving on from Survival and Denial, after many attempts, and I never went back to Richard.

The Day I Decided to End it All
Fast forward quite a few years. A lot had happened and I had worked hard to make progress. But life wasn't easy, and I found myself back

in a place where I didn't think I had the strength to go on.

Over the years, one thing has remained the same: I have always relied on my ability to work my ass off. I may not always be the smartest person in a room, but I can be counted on to be one of the hardest working. After a car accident ten months earlier that left me in physical and speech therapy, I was back to doing what I had to do to survive. I found a job I could do—delivering newspapers. I was also working part-time for an insurance salesman doing mailings three days a week (He always said I was way over-qualified for that job). Eventually, I was waitressing at night at Fox & Hound and, three days a week, during lunch, I was waitressing at Applebee's down the road.

Guess where I was. I was right back in the World of Survival.

See a pattern here? One thing I did have enough sense to do was to start college. There was a small voice inside that ached for something more and, while my head didn't believe I could become more, my heart did. So, for some reason, I listened to my heart. In between all the jobs, I was taking classes. I was just getting back on my feet. I was exhausted, but with the insurance payment that took months to receive from the car accident, I paid back almost everyone who helped me during the previous ten months. I had paid the doctor bills and even moved into a duplex with my three children. I only slept four hours a night on average, but I was moving forward.

I had an old Grand Prix that had been given to me after that accident. The mirror was held on by duct tape (the bumper too), but I didn't care how beat up it was. I was so thankful for it and the friends who gave it to me. It allowed me to have a sense of success again. That vehicle allowed me to *feel* like a good mom again. It gave me a little dose of hope that I could provide for my kids again.

I was driving home from a late night shift at Fox & the Hound, around 1:00 a.m. The county was fixing the road (partly because of my accident) and had the lanes redirected (four lanes down to two). At the exact point where I had the accident, there was a great big pothole. Bam! I hit it, and my right front tire blew. In a matter of seconds… boom! My right rear tire popped. There I was, stranded on a dark highway with no lights, no cell phone, a little tip money, and I had to deliver newspapers in just four hours.

I looked up at the sky crying and screaming, with tears flowing down my face. "What do you want from me?"

> *I looked up at the sky, crying and screaming, with tears flowing down my face. "What do you want from me?"*

In that moment, my soul died, and I was done. Done! No more just surviving! Done with being tired! Done with working my ass off! Done! I just didn't have it in me to keep going. Why was all of this happening to me?

I debated in my head what I should do. Should I stay there until morning and wait for the rush hour? Should I start walking and hope there was a house within a couple of miles?

Thirty minutes later, as I looked into the rear view mirror, in the distance, there were headlights heading in my direction. I watched as they got closer and then they took a bounce and then another quick bounce. The car came to a stop right behind mine. A gentleman in a BMW was now in the same situation as me: stuck with two popped tires.

As he got out of his car, he too was yelling a few choice words. I waited for him, and he approached my door. We had an exchange as I told him it had just happened to me too and I had no way of getting ahold of anyone. Thankfully, he had a cell phone and let me use it. A cousin had been staying with us for a week as she looked at colleges in Nebraska. I gave her a call to tell her what happened and that I needed a ride.

That could have been such a pivotal moment in my life, but instead of turning to the Lord, Allah, or any other God, I didn't. I went running the other way. I didn't drive straight to hell, but my plan was to find the road that went there.

On that dark, painful, lonely night, I made the decision. It was so clear and a "peace" filled my heart.

As soon as my kids graduated from high school, I was going to take my own life.

It wasn't that I was thinking about how the kids would feel or what they would do without me when I was gone. I very quickly had a plan, and a strategy, a reasoning if you will. I did want to make sure they were old enough, so they could handle life on their own. I wasn't going to leave them unexpectedly. I would make sure they were young adults first.

I just couldn't take any more obstacles or challenges. I could not start my life next Monday, or any other day for that matter, again.

When you get to that point of desperation, you convince yourself that nobody is going to care if you're there or not. Not that they didn't love me, but everyone would actually be better off if I was gone.

It was hard to breathe. It was getting harder to believe there was a purpose for me. I was so tired.

I lost the will to live.

So often people say that others who take their lives are so selfish. I see it from a different standpoint. They're so tired, so alone, they actually think they're helping by not being a problem anymore. If you have never been that lonely, desperate, or tired, you will never understand. My heart wants to cry out when people accuse suicide victims of being selfish. I don't believe in suicide, and I am not condoning it. But if you haven't been there, you can't possibly know what they are feeling.

Even though I didn't have a relationship with God, I was religious. I was more afraid of going to hell than of actually dying. (More on that in my next book.) Killing myself, ending my life, was the only goal I had the strength to make. It was the only goal I could see. Nothing I planned for myself had ever come to fruition. The only hope I had was to make it three more years, so I could go through with my Final Exit Plan.

I went back and forth between the Survival Stage and Denial Stage for the next three years. I was in complete Denial of my talents, strengths, and the ability to make it through. If I hadn't felt so defeated and exhausted, I might have been able to look back at everything I'd already survived and realized there was hope. But I just couldn't see it.

When Denial Hits Home

It's one thing for adults to be in Denial but, when our children are living in the Denial Stage, it can be devastating if nothing is done.

My son Josh, now 17, had been living with his dad. At one point he had been working at Taco Bell for three days. This job was a huge step for him as he had struggled the past couple years since his father and I had divorced. Three days into that job, he quit. Then he called to tell me. I couldn't believe it. I had been on his case so many times. When was he going to grow up?

"Joshua, you need to step up," I told him. "Your dad needs you to help. You can't work at a job for three days and quit."

Josh was in major Denial that his father was in poor health and was going to be unable to continue working.

What I didn't know was that Josh was literally going crazy and had two holes in his brain from the use of street drugs for the prior three years.

Josh had been struggling with his father's alcoholism for years, and he also had a really hard time dealing with our divorce. A couple years earlier, he decided to live with his father. In my heart I knew this could not end well. Two co-dependent people living in the same house never does. But, when they are teenagers, they get to choose.

That day, he sounded more angry than normal. More frustrated than normal. When we finally ended the conversation, I looked at my now-husband, "Something is not right. He's so angry. He's going to hurt Will."

Two hours later, I got a call from one of my daughters. "Mom, Josh just tried to kill Dad!"

They say that mothers have an intuition that defies explanation. I had experienced it that day. My heart sank and my head dropped.

Josh had started beating his father with the phone after we hung up. He then proceeded with a shotgun and put it to his head.

Something stopped him from putting the shell in, so he flipped the gun around and started beating his dad with it.

My Life Begins Next Monday...

...he flipped the gun around and started beating his dad...

Later we got Josh some help and found out he has a disorder called Paranoid Schizophrenia with Thought Broadcasting. Thought Broadcasting is when a person thinks everyone else knows what he is thinking. Which then begs the question, why should they have to explain anything? It's very frustrating when you believe everyone knows your every thought and you have to constantly be repeating yourself.

This is an extreme example of how living in the Denial Stage can snowball. Here is what I have learned: if we don't accept our circumstances, it can lead to violence, self-injury, isolation, depression, and so much more. I've spoken with people who are cutters. People who intentionally cut themselves. One has shared that he lived in Denial. Denial of his situation. Denial that he has any control over his life and actions.

Abused children live in Denial (unintentionally) and have no idea how other people live. I was in Denial about my second husband, Will, Josh's father. Will loved me and he loved the kids, but only to his ability, which was low. He wasn't a man with a high inner drive. He was the 9-5, keep to himself, eat dinner at 6:00, be drunk by 7:00, pass out by 8:00 type. He was somebody who let me do what I wanted without questioning and knew I would take care of him. Not a healthy relationship in any form.

I thought I could motivate him to want more out of life, more for our family, more for him. But, I couldn't change him. I lived in the Denial Stage the whole 13 years we were together.

It was Josh's situation that forced me to leave the Survival Stage and the Denial Stage. I had to move to the Acceptance Stage in many areas of my life.

The sooner you can accept the alternative, the reality, the better off you are. I look around now and see people living in the Survival Stage and Denial Stage everywhere. Their eyes reflect the questions they ask themselves every night. "Why am I here and why can't I have more?"

Denial in the Business World
Denial showed up in my career as well. You see, you are who you are…all…day…long. You cannot be one way at work and then one way at home. Which is why Denial is a big problem in the business world too.

I can't tell you how many times I've seen Denial play out in corporate America. Salespeople who say they want something more in their lives, but they have all these expectations of the company, and they're not accepting the fact that they have to go earn it. Are there cases where the company or a boss could do more? Absolutely. Are there bosses or supervisors who are in the wrong position? Absolutely. But let's go with the majority here (I am guessing over 80%). They're in Denial of their situation, what they have/don't have, their skills, and their ability to make decisions.

People living in this kind of Denial don't only struggle with it in their personal lives, they struggle with it in their business lives as well. They don't know what they don't know. They don't have what it takes to move forward with any consistency. They seem to get stuck.

> *People living in this kind of Denial don't only struggle with it in their personal lives, they struggle with it in their business lives as well.*

Bottom line. When we choose not to accept something, that is Denial. There are pros and cons to every stage and the pro to the Denial stage is that it helps us not get hurt. It's the same in our professional lives. It enables us to deal with situations later, when we are able.

For example, you know you need to deal with the long-term

training of your team, but the current moment requires you to hire three more people and get them up and running. Some may call this prioritizing. It is, except to do long-term training, you would have to assess your current employees and possibly deal with their personal needs in order to create a long-term training agenda. This could open up a whole new box of worms you can't deal with right now. In this situation, living in the Denial Stage may be required for a short term.

It's not just struggling businesspeople though; I've met some very successful people who have ended up in Denial. Many of them have been blinded by their success. They don't feel it is their responsibility to keep learning or growing. They have a title and, for whatever reason, they have come to believe their title means entitlement. That is a form of Denial. When it's time to make a change, they just can't choose to do it. No matter how obvious it becomes, they are blind or paralyzed by the changing world.

I was in the car industry for nine years. During that time, newspapers were just starting to go out of business, and the whole country (and the world) was transitioning to the dot com era. For eight years, I walked into 300+ car dealerships a year as part of my job responsibility. We had so many dealerships in complete Denial about the Internet era. They had no idea how—and no desire—to change. They had convinced themselves the Internet was just a fad that would go away. They were determined to stick to their guns, wait it out, and stay with their old, comfortable ways of doing business.

(The Internet going away? Can you even imagine?)

Part of my job was teaching them that, if they didn't accept this new era of the World Wide Web, *they* were the ones that were going to go away, because the Internet was here to stay.

I had one particular region (NC, SC, VA, and PA) where more car dealerships went out of business that year than in any other region in the U.S. When these dealerships didn't transition to Acceptance, they didn't choose to go forward; they went back into Denial and tried to do things that same old way. And it didn't work. And they got left behind.

So, see? These principles apply to business just like they do to individuals. If your business or career is stuck in the Survival stage or Denial stage, and you can't seem to move to Acceptance (without sliding back) and then move forward into the other stages, you won't ever experience success consistently. You'll become just another failure, another statistic.

But you don't have to become a statistic. You have the power to change. The choice is up to you. You just have to take that big leap of faith; take one step each day; own up to your circumstances; recognize them for what they are; and make a plan to get out of them.

And work your tail off to get you from point A to point B.

You can do this, friend.

My Life Begins Next Monday...

THE APPLICATION BLUEPRINT

1. Take a moment and think about two times you had trouble accepting a situation.

Example: I had a hard time accepting _____.

Personal:
1._____
2._____
3._____

Career:
1._____
2._____
3._____

2. What were the top three reasons it was hard to accept?

Personal:
1._____
2._____
3._____

Career:
1._____
2._____
3._____

3. Now ask yourself: "What did I learn?"

The answer will give you direction for your next step.

Personal Situation:

I learned _____

Career Situation:

I learned _____

4. How can you recognize when you are feeling stuck or unable to make a decision?

Personal: _____
_____
_____
_____
_____

Career:_____
_____
_____
_____
_____

THE TAKEAWAY

What is one thing you can take away from this chapter and apply to your personal life?

_____
_____
_____

What is one thing you can take away from this chapter and apply to your business or career?

_____
_____
_____

What is one tangible, practical thing you can do today that will make a difference tomorrow?

_____
_____
_____

Shari Strong

Denial

*I don't know
Not much is true.
The illusions of grandeur
It's not me; it's you.*

*Scared and alone
It doesn't matter.
The future is now.
The seconds are scattered.*

*One step forward.
One step back.
It's a game
Not a track.*

*Don't feel.
Don't commit to something more.
Why?
I can't take anymore.*

Chapter 3: Acceptance

You either walk inside your story and own it or you stand outside your story and hustle for your worthiness.

−Brene Brown

3

The Acceptance stage is the most dangerous stage of all. So much hangs in the balance here. It's ultimately about making a decision. We've got to either move forward, or we're going to go sliding back.

I've seen it happen so many times. It's happened to me. Maybe it's happened to you. Or someone you love. If you've watched friends or family get to the Acceptance stage, then go flying back through Denial to Survival, it's tough. Chances are you got frustrated and angry with them for going back.

I get it. I really do.

The Acceptance stage is the most dangerous stage of all.

The Tough Work of Acceptance
Here's the thing. If someone has been in the Survival Stage for a long time, they've figured out how to survive there. It might not be any fun, but they know how to do it. Now they have to go survive somewhere else? Think about what you're asking here. You want them to leave what they know with no guarantee they'll be doing anything more than just surviving again? But in a new, unknown place this time?

Well, that's change, and that's work, and that's scary.

And it may seem unreasonable to you, but it's harder than you can imagine if you haven't lived it yourself.

To move from Survival to Denial to Acceptance you've got to convince yourself that where you're headed will be better, and make you happier, than where you're coming from. You have to convince yourself that, just like you learned to survive where you were, you'll learn how to survive where you're going. You have to become so irritated and tired of where you are that you move forward out of a feeling of *enough is enough*. Then, eventually, you'll do more than survive; you'll thrive.

> *Then, eventually, you'll do more than survive; you'll thrive.*

If we can't/won't do this, we'll go back to living in Denial. So many people do. It's easier. It's more comfortable. It's what we know.

That's why I had not one, but two, alcoholic husbands. Instead of accepting who I was and could be, I became a glutton for punishment, defining myself by the broken men I married. I let my past truly define who I was destined to be.

My whole life I hungered to be accepted. If you don't accept yourself for who you are, if you don't like yourself or the decisions you have made, then how will anyone else? More importantly, *why* would anyone else? I had heard that cliché so many times and never understood it. I always had a positive exterior, even with the life I was leading. I always had a smile on my face. I was always nice to others. I loved my kids. Isn't that what loving yourself meant? Putting on an act?

No. That's not it at all.

It took me years to learn the next point.

> *If we don't accept ourselves, what does that mean?*

If we don't accept ourselves, what does that mean? It means rejection. We reject ourselves, which is the ultimate Denial. We reject who we are meant to be. We reject who and what our soul is meant to be.

We reject others who look like or have what we want. Understanding rejection is what will help you move to Acceptance.

After my divorce from my second husband, I realized I had to start taking responsibility for my own life beyond working hard. I had to take responsibility for the decisions I had made, and I had to let go of people I had listened to in the past. If I was going to change my future, I had to change my actions. I had to accept my part in creating my life to this point and accept my responsibility moving forward.

One of the most negative influencers in my life, at the time, was my mother. We had never gotten along. Now, this is not an *It's My Parent's Fault* section. I only want to paint a picture of how learned behavior influences our thought patterns, our decision-making processes, and ultimately how we move from stage to stage. I want to raise your awareness because, ultimately, if I was going to do more, be more, and have more, it was up to me. The same is true for you.

My mother and I had never had a great relationship. I remember always feeling like she hated me. We never showed love in a physical sense with hugging or even with our words. I never knew why though.

Think back to when you were 10 years old. Where were you? Ten is when dreams for the future are in full bloom. My dream was to be a superstar. Yes, I was going to be the next Cher…E! I would sit in my room for hours listening to Peaches and Herb on my pink record player. *Reunited and it feels so good, reunited and we understood…* I would get so moved and inspired I would write three or four songs in one evening. I knew that someday I would inspire millions of people with *my* music, and that was *my* purpose.

I just knew.

One evening, I wrote *the* song. It was the first one I was ready to share with the world. Imagine a child excited after they discover something or learn something for the first time and running to their parent. I jumped up and ran. "Mom, Mom! You have to read this! I wrote a song!"

She grabbed the paper and took a brief glance at it. Then she ripped the paper into shreds and said with disgust, "Shari, you are just a dreamer, and dreamers never get anything. You will never have a house; you will never have a family; and you need to just quit dreaming."

Shari Strong

"Dreamers never get anything. You will never have a house. You will never have a family. You'll never have anything. Quit dreaming!"

Have you ever had a dream crushed? Have you ever had someone tell you that you couldn't do something or that you'd never amount to anything? Interestingly enough, I didn't cry. I actually remember feeling sorry for her. While she never won Mother of the Year, my instincts at 10 told me she was unhappy.

But I decided right then and there that I wasn't doomed to the same unhappiness.

That wasn't the first time she transferred how she was feeling onto me, and it wasn't the last. Years later, we had an on-again off-again relationship and, at 33, I remember the last time I cried over her. The last time I wished my mother would be proud of me. The last time I was going to wonder why I wasn't "good enough for her to love."

There was bickering going on in my extended family. When my aunt passed away, instead of coming together, my family divided. I was disappointed but not surprised. Our history as a family was jam-packed with issues and arguments that were never addressed or forgiven, competition, dislike of in-laws, and all the things that complicate family relationships.

In this particular season of unrest, my mother and I were in an off-season. So much so that she hadn't even acknowledged my children, her grandchildren, for over two years. Then, out of the blue, all three of my children received a Christmas card from her with money inside. Needless to say, I didn't trust her motives.

Long story short, the argument was over my grandmother and the amount given at Christmas to some grandchildren and not others. I decided I was not going to be a pawn in the drama again and sent all three cards back. Then I received this:

Dear Miss [my second husband's last name],
You don't know how to have a relationship. You have been divorced twice. I have been married for 36 years. I won't die a lonely person. I have brothers and sister-in-laws who love me. A son and daughter in law, and a wonderful daughter across the street, 4 (she didn't include my three children in the count), wonderful grandkids and some great friends that I've had for 30 or more years, more than you can say. I don't want you at my funeral when I do leave this world, because you are not anything to me. You can think whatever you want to think of me. I have plenty of people, I love, even though you say my heart doesn't love. It does, just NOT YOU!

The ultimate rejection. *I know how to love, just not you!*

The ultimate rejection. "I know how to love, just not you!"

This was how I learned to communicate with family and friends throughout my childhood and into my thirties. If you don't do what I like, there will be hell to pay. I had to finally accept that my mom could not give me what I needed. After all these years, I finally understand why she behaved the way she did. (That is a whole 'nother book.) I believe, deep down, she never accepted who she was or what she had. So, it was always everyone else's job to make her feel good, make her feel wanted, give her what she needed.

Ironically, it was just this past year that I received a birthday card out of the blue from her. She is in her sixties now, so my hope is this is a sincere attempt to have a relationship. We have even met. Bottom line: even if she hasn't changed, I have accepted her for who she is, and she will have to accept me. I can't change her, and I stopped hating her years ago, but more importantly I have forgiven her.

Because of that, now I can accept *me*.

We have to suck it up, look in the mirror, and accept the cards we've been dealt (or the mess we've gotten ourselves into), so we can begin to grow. We don't necessarily have to *fix* ourselves at this point; we've just got to raise our awareness of our reality. We have to accept how things are before we can change them.

Acceptance is hard, but it's the most crucial step to moving forward into all you can be. It's not your mother's fault; it's not your father's fault; it's not your husband's fault; it's not the economy's fault, etc. You are right where you are supposed to be in this life, based on the decisions you made (even in situations out of your control).

The kicker? Tomorrow you will be too. So, what can you do today?

John Maxwell's Law of Process

John Maxwell's Law of Process states: *Leadership develops daily, not in a day*. What does this have to do with accepting who we are? We lead ourselves first before we can lead others. But to accept anything means we have to be willing to learn. Here are the levels of awareness John teaches. We all go through each of these levels in life or when we are learning anything new:

1. I don't know what I don't know.
2. I know that I need to know.
3. I know what I don't know.
4. I know and grow and it starts to show.
5. I simply go forward because I want to know.

Notice how these levels encompass Denial, Acceptance, and moving forward in Confidence.

One step that changed my world was the process of self discovery and life coaching training in 2011. While earning my Life Coaching Certificate through IPEC School of Coaching, I was required to take an Energy Leadership Assessment. I thought it was going to be some foo-foo, the universe is in control, type of thing. Was I wrong!

They teach the 7 levels of energy and how we make it through each day based on our emotional actions and reactions. It was the light bulb moments that helped me finally mature into an adult. If you are dedicated to learning how and why you do the things you do, this is for you. It showed me that I was making the majority of decisions, even at work, from a place of victim thinking. No wonder, when things didn't go my way, I went into negative thinking and negative talking.

It was the first assessment that didn't just put a label on me; it gave me hope and a process to recognize why and when I tended to operate in that mode. It showed me that every moment is an attitude opportunity.

Go to www.MyLifeBeginsNextMonday.com and you can get your free copy of the 7 levels of energy.

Attitude Opportunity
Attitude Opportunity is a theme running through my life even today. It's more than just looking at the bright side of things or making lemonade when life hands you lemons. It's about truly acknowledging that something might not be that great (and maybe it's downright awful), giving yourself a short period of time to be sad and/or angry, and then asking yourself, "What is the opportunity here?"

Then you make this a habit. Whenever something difficult comes your way, you force yourself to ask, "What is the opportunity here?"

And, before you know it, this will come naturally. And when you begin to see how hard times often birth times of growth and potential and joy, you learn to embrace those hard times with anticipation. How will God use this in my life to make me a better person? I can't wait to see!

Maybe a child with special needs is an opportunity for you to learn patience. Perhaps getting fired from your job will be an opportunity for an even better one. Maybe the loss of a loved one will give you the opportunity to comfort others who face loss.

Why do some people have to struggle while others seem to sail right through?

I've never understood why life is harder for some people than others. Why do some people have to struggle while others seem to sail right through? It's just not fair, is it?

Like I mentioned in Chapter 1, I've learned that comparing your life to others doesn't help anything. I suggest a twist, putting a positive spin on your struggles. Say to yourself, "The more challenging my life is, the stronger I'll be. Bring it."

Trials are a filter of life. A way of filtering out who has the strength to carry out larger missions in the future. Some say it is karma; good things come back to those who handle situations well.

In the business world, those in charge will often watch to see how people react under pressure or in the midst of turmoil to determine who can take on more responsibility in the way of a promotion. So challenges and hardships can be a good, good thing.

In fact, may I be so bold as to suggest that, if your life is (and has always been) carefree and easy, you just might be missing out?

Every moment you are given is an attitude opportunity.

Every moment you are given is an *attitude opportunity*.
What are you going to do with it?

It's Really Up to You
Working up the courage to leave Richard was a necessary step for me to move on to the positive stages of Acceptance, Confidence,

Connection, and Grace. I totally get that sometimes you have to leave something completely. Sometimes you just have to break free and get out.

The Law of Magnetism states: "You don't get what you want; you get who you are." In a similar vein, I once read this statement, and it stuck with me: "The truth is, our lives are not just a reflection of what happens to us. They are a reflection of what we make happen."

It was such a series of slow baby steps for me. Being able to see beyond the moment I was living. I couldn't see myself deserving more, just a little bit more. I wasn't dreaming. I was still living in the Survival Stage and the Denial Stage. Jumping back and forth.

This was the first time I allowed myself to take a tiny step into the Acceptance Stage. I started to accept a little bit that I had to move on. When we find a way to persevere, when we start to accept who we are, then we can start to connect with others. We'll talk more about Connection (oh, it's so important) in Chapter 6.

I once met a gentleman who had lost his wife five years earlier. He shared with me how he felt when his wife died. He was a successful business owner with two grown sons who were following in his footsteps. He wasn't old enough to retire but felt like he had just been surviving for the last five years.

When I asked him, "If you could do anything at this point, what would it be?" he started to tear up. He said he really hadn't thought about moving forward in that way. He was always asking himself the question, "What will I do without her?" And it was a question he didn't want to answer, didn't know how to answer.

"I guess I haven't really accepted her death yet," he said, "and haven't been willing to ask myself different questions."

This is another example of how each stage drives our behaviors. Eventually he will figure out what motivates him, or he will go back to the Denial stage and live there. Every now and again, he will use a behavior he learned when he was still in the Survival Stage to get through the day.

I hope and pray he is able to move forward into the next stages—for his family and for himself.

Shari Strong

Starting to Dream
Three years ago, after we moved into a new house, I found a book I had read in back in 1996. Keep in mind, at this time, I was on food stamps, didn't have much money, had just gotten my GED, hadn't even thought about college yet, was still with my 2nd husband, my kids were 5, 6, and 7, and we were living in a trailer

My circumstances hadn't really changed that much. The only difference was this: I was allowing myself to dream, to imagine what my life could actually look like. I had just gotten promoted to manager for the first time in my life for the National Federation of Independent Business, so I was dreaming about what I could have if I kept moving forward.

The book was titled *Why Not Me?* The authors were Paul and Dan Monahan, two Tony Robbins-type brothers who were gurus in leadership and were doing what I am attempting to do—influence the way people think and act, so they can do more, be more, and have more. One of the assignments in the book was to write down 20 things you want in your life in the future.

When I found this book again in 2011 (15 years later) and read that list, I was shocked and thrilled to discover that 14 of my 20 dreams had come true (and the rest no longer mattered to me). A few of them had taken a slightly different twist, but I still counted them.

I don't know about you, but I think that's pretty amazing. Indulge me as we take a look at that list. (And remember what you've learned about my story so far. It certainly wasn't pretty.)

As you read, begin thinking about your own dreams. If I can accomplish my dreams, so you can you!

20 Things I Want to Have, Do, or Be (circa 1996)
This list is a treasure to me, and I'm so glad I found it after so many years. It's a testimony to the power of dreaming big way before your dreams have any likelihood of becoming reality.

Here are 20 things I dreamed for my future almost 20 years ago:

1. *Own a part in Tony Robbins' Destiny.* (I'm part of the John Maxwell Team, so close enough in my book. No pun intended.)

2. *Own a Land Rover*. (I don't own a Land Rover, but I do own a Hummer—an H3. Check.)

3. *Own my dream house*. (I've owned two dream houses. I live in one right now. On a golf course. On a lake. In the mountains.)

6. *Stay in the shape I'm in*. (Check. After three babies, I'm actually at the same weight I was in high school and wear the same size.)

8. *Take the kids to two cities a year*. (In my last job, I took each of my kids to a city twice a year, so check.)

9. *Speak and help a thousand people in a year*. (See, it was always my dream to be a speaker. I achieved that goal last year.)

10. *Member of a golf course*. (Not only am I a member, I live on a golf course. Back in 1996, I had never golfed a day in my life, but I must have had the idea that, if you were a member of a golf course, you were successful.)

11. *Go on a mission trip*. (I went on my first mission trip to Guatemala a couple years ago.)

14. *Own my own airplane*. (We don't yet, but it's in the works. My husband and his pilot friend are researching the airplane recovery business, and we'd have to own an airplane for the business.)

15. *Give $10,000 a year to my church*. (We didn't give $10,000, but we gave more last year than we've ever given to charities with the promise of an even bigger year this year.)

17. *Always be open for my kids*. (My kids will tell you they can always come to me about anything. I have a great relationship with them.)

18. *Work out every day at my home gym*. (Okay, so not every day. And I don't have a gym. But I do have an elliptical in my office.)

19. *Be aware of my future*. (I teach people how to be aware of their futures. In fact, this is a huge part of my passion, purpose, and vision statements.)

20. *Always be grateful*. (I take time every day to make sure I acknowledge how grateful I am to the Lord.)

Once you move past Survival and Denial and accept things for what they are, you can start to dream. And then it's only a matter of time (and a lot of hard work) before they come true.

Success in 4D
I spend a lot of time sharing my Success in 4D Program with captive audiences. The 4 D's = Define It, Decide It, Design It, Do It. And time and time again, when I ask them which is the hardest of the 4 D's, 80% of them say, "Do It."

Would you agree, or would you choose a different D?

"Do It" seems logical, but it's not a true statement. Doing it isn't the hardest. Designing the plan isn't the hardest. Deciding to do it is the second hardest part, but defining what it is you want to do? That's hard.

The day I finally decided to make a plan to leave my dream job, defining what I really wanted was the hardest part. I had just graduated college at the age of 40. I had just achieved my Life Coaching certificate. I had just started on the John Maxwell team. I was sitting on the couch and looked at my husband and said, "What am I waiting for?"

He said, "I don't know."

"I think I could be a great coach, speaker, and trainer," I told him. "That's what I've done my whole life. I think I could go do that for myself and help others above and beyond any company."

Once I was able to define what I really wanted (and that was the hardest part—it took me 40+ years to figure out what I really wanted), it was scary because I had to decide to do it.

Fear is an unpleasant emotion caused by the belief that something or someone is dangerous, likely to cause pain, or is a threat. If we fear we're in danger or about to get hurt, it's pretty hard to keep defining who we are and what we want. Or we know there will be obstacles and pain, but we have to decide to do it anyway.

That's what I did. I designed a two-year plan; we saved up money; I knew what I was going to do; and I resigned on the day I said I was going to do it. Like they say, "good is the enemy of great," but I now say, "great is the enemy of getting started." Just get started!

You've moved from the Survival Stage to the Denial Stage and taken the big leap to the Acceptance Stage. Next we'll talk about figuring out what motivates you so you can take more steps forward into Confidence.

This is the exciting part, friends!

My Life Begins Next Monday...

THE APPLICATION BLUEPRINT

1. Take a moment and think about two times in which you had a hard time accepting a situation.

Example: I had a hard time accepting _____.

Personal:
1._____
2._____
3._____

Career:
1._____
2._____
3._____

2. What were the top three reasons it was hard to accept?

Personal:
1._____
2._____
3._____

Career:
1._____
2._____
3._____

3. Now ask yourself: "What did I learn?" The answer will give you direction for your next step.

Personal Situation:

I learned:
_____
_____
_____

Career Situation:

I learned:
_____
_____
_____

4. How can you recognize when you are feeling stuck or unable to make a decision?

Personal: _____
_____
_____
_____
_____

Career:_____
_____
_____
_____
_____

My Life Begins Next Monday...

5. Read this and then follow the directions:

Imagine it is five years from today. What year is it?
Imagine what your kids will look like.
Image what your spouse will look like.
What will be the number you have in your bank account?
What will your title be at your place of work?
What is the biggest thing you will have accomplished, looking back?

Close your eyes and take 3 minutes to visualize the above and any other goals you have for the next five years.

Write those goals here.

1. _____
2. _____
3. _____
4. _____
5. _____
6. _____

THE TAKEAWAY

What is one thing you can take away from this chapter and apply to your personal life?
_____
_____
_____

What is one thing you can take away from this chapter and apply to your business or career?
_____
_____
_____

What is one tangible, practical thing you can do today that will make a difference tomorrow?
_____
_____
_____

My Life Begins Next Monday...

The Ledge

*Frustrations of the day
Don't get washed away.
It's a wasteland of thought
protecting my mind from rot.*

*It's a will known beyond this earth
Checking in from my perch.
I take a breath and hold it in
To only feel the wind begin.*

*Lagging behind is what I feel
The race for hope and only to use my will
The characters in my head
We all want to be led.*

*What I started with today
Has changed with one play.
It's a reality with an edge
My hope of getting off this ledge.*

Chapter 4: Motivation

Ability is what you're capable of doing. Motivation determines what you do. Attitude determines how well you do it.

-Lou Holtz

4

It took a devastating car accident to help me recognize what really motivates me in life. Isn't life just like that sometimes? We need a huge jolt to knock us upside the head and get us moving in a different direction.

It's tempting to want to skip straight to the Confidence Stage at this point, but we can't forget this all-important stage of Motivation. Figuring out what motivates you, what drives you, what makes you *you,* will help you determine what you truly want out of life. And it will ensure that you set off down the path that will take you there.

What's My Motivation Here?
It was 2003. I was in the middle of divorce #2 and raising three teenagers with no child support. In spite of that, I was doing well for myself. My kids were provided for, and I was working hard and meeting success.

It was 11:59 on a beautiful Friday morning. The sun was shining; I was driving my minivan (which I loved); and all was right with the world (relatively speaking). A car was stopped facing me, waiting to cross the highway I was driving on. Just as I was about to pass by, BAM! The car had pulled in front of me, and I slammed into it. As I gripped the steering wheel, the airbag deployed. My forehead met the airbag, and the airbag won.

I saw nothing but white clouds. My mind scrambled to make sense of what was happening. Commotion ensued. Lights and sirens blared from fire trucks and police cars. Yet no one came to help me. It felt like an out-of-body experience. After a moment that felt like eternity, I began yelling, "I'm in here! I'm in here!"

This particular spot on the Nebraska highway (heading from Omaha to Blair) was the scene of many accidents over the years. Time and time again the county had considered widening the road to fix the problem blind spot. It wasn't until my accident that construction was finally approved.

A young man, in his twenties, had run into the back of the car, forcing them in front of me. In a blink of an eye, I hit that car. My van spun around and into their lane and, lo and behold, I was hit again, in the backside of my van.

My life as I knew it was forever changed.

It could have been anyone that day. The young man wasn't drunk or on drugs. He wasn't driving recklessly or texting. It was an accident.

Because of the airbag impact, I sustained neck and facial injuries that went beyond whiplash and cuts and bruises. The car accident affected me physically and mentally. During the three weeks following the accident, I was sore and suffered from headaches, but I felt lucky. I thought I was home free.

A few weeks after the accident, my children and I were invited to a friend's house for Easter brunch. On the way there, in our new vehicle on loan from a local dealer, my daughter, Ambir, said, "Mom, what is wrong with your face?"

"What do you mean?" I said.

"Your face looks funny," she said.

I looked in the mirror, and sure enough, she was right. The right side of my face was drooping. Soon, my tongue starting doing things of its own accord, like sticking out of my mouth. Then my head started bobbing slightly.

You've got to be kidding me, I thought. I could no longer control my own tongue or head? I thought I was having a stroke. When we arrived at the brunch, a few friends went with me to the hospital. They ran some tests and sent me home. "You're stressed," they said.

This went on for six weeks. Just stress? I don't think so. Finally, I found a doctor who was able to diagnose my problem.

Oral Mandibular Dystonia—uncontrollable movements of the head, jaw, and tongue. My face no longer belonged to me. I couldn't make it do what I wanted it to do. I was put on medicine that calmed and controlled nerves. Between stress and the impact of the airbag to my head causing it to jolt back violently, the nerves in my neck were jacked, to say the least.

The young man was insured, but he had a policy with the lowest limits for a vehicle that was paid off. I met with multiple accident-chasing attorneys, and every single one of them insisted I needed to sue him to cover the health care costs, the loss of income, and pain and suffering. I had to leave my sales job, as I couldn't speak correctly, and this was going to be major rehab.

The question I kept asking myself, and eventually the attorneys, was, "If I sue, and we win, where will this young man get the money to pay me?"

The answer I received was, "His parents would have to mortgage their home. Or he could make me monthly payments for the rest of his life. "This isn't your problem to worry about," they all said as a matter of fact. "It's his."

No matter how much this had messed up my life, I couldn't justify ruining his as well!

I didn't agree. No matter how humiliating and debilitating my injuries were, and how much this had messed up my life, I couldn't justify ruining his as well! I held so much power in my hands, and life hadn't been kind to me to this point. This could be a meal ticket, even if I didn't heal fully. But was it worth it?

At the time, I didn't know why I had the intuition to not sue, but I didn't want to wield power and opportunity to make money in this way. What kind of message would I be sending to my teenagers if I sued this young man? What if something similar happened to one of them someday? What if someone sued them and made them pay for it for the rest of their lives?

Looking back, I realize my #1 motivator in life, influence, was unconsciously activated. I wasn't motivated by the money I could get from this. A voice kept whispering that it wasn't right to get rich off some settlement, especially if insurance couldn't cover it. I had a chance to influence this young man's life for positive, and influence the future of his story (as well as my own) by how I handled this.

Influence is something I value highly, take very seriously, and it has ultimately shaped decisions throughout my life.

I told my lawyer, "I'm not going to sue."

The 7 Different Types of Motivation
Are you aware of the different types of Motivation? I'm intrigued by them, and I think you will be too. We're all motivated by each one in some way but, for most of us, one or two rise to the top.

This is so important as you move on. Once you accept where you are, you have to focus on the future so you don't go back to Denial. This is the best way I have found to start moving forward. Some of my friends have gone to therapy at this point. Let me be clear: I am not saying therapy doesn't work; I just feel many of us could move on if we would focus on the future, not the past. Therapy seems to be more effective when we are in Survival, Denial, or Acceptance Stages. Unfortunately, that is when it is toughest for someone to make that decision.

This is when you want to learn *why* you do what you do, not based on the past, but based on what you want in the future. It's the difference between driving forward by looking in the rearview mirror or using the rearview mirror to glance back as a precaution every now and again.

There are seven motivations I learned from a coach, and I believe they are valid. They are in line with Maslow's Hierarchy of Needs. As you read these, ask yourself, "What gets me out of bed in the morning?"

1. **Social Motivation.**

This has to do with the need to belong and be accepted by others. The underlying drive comes from socio-cultural influences that make someone want to achieve a goal. People who are motivated socially want everyone to be invited to the party. And show up! They do not necessarily need to be the life of the party, but they want everyone there and having fun.

2. **Money Motivation.**

This motivator is pretty straightforward. People who are motivated by money usually put a dollar value on anything they do. They don't just say the cliché *time is money*, they mean it and live it. Donald Trump may come to mind. He has made money, lost it, and made it again. Whether you like him or not, his ability to do what he does proves that, when someone is working and living in their strengths, playing to their true motivation, it works!

3. Achievement Motivation.

You'll know this is one of your top motivators if you want to be the best, even if there is no ribbon or award involved (that's recognition motivation). People who are achievement motivated take the test, and *want* to get a 100 on the test even if they are the only person taking it and no one else will know. The person motivated by achievement seeks to attain set goals. They are the list makers and check things off and don't feel gratified unless they are all done. They like feedback/progress reports along the way to ensure they are on track to reach their goal(s). One criticism of achievement-oriented individuals is that, because they assume everyone is as driven as they are, they can be demanding of others. The second criticism: they have tunnel vision.

4. Recognition Motivation.

This particular type of motivation is based on the premise that we all want to be recognized for our work and/or contributions. This is the person who takes the test, gets a 100, and *wants* the blue ribbon. One thing to keep in mind about this form of motivation, though, is that everyone doesn't like to be recognized in the same manner. For example, while one person may revel in being recognized at a fancy banquet thrown in their honor, another might quiver in nervous fear at the very thought of being rewarded so publicly. People who are motivated by recognition often get a bad rap—especially in sales organizations where achievement of goals is expected, as they are seen as high maintenance or needy. If you are motivated by recognition, own it! Many times, it doesn't take much, just a thank you. I have found that those who are not motivated by this have a hard time giving it, especially when in a leadership role. If you have a child or an employee who is motivated by recognition, give it to them!

5. Influence Motivation.

This has to do with being able to impact situations or people in a way that brings about change. This change can take many forms: a change in behavior, attitude, goals, values, organizational structure, etc. One key factor to note here: to be able to influence doesn't necessarily mean you have power. Responsibility is another form of influence when it comes to this motivator. Someone involved in a Big Brother or Big Sister program may be an example of being motivated by influence. Most speakers are not motivated by fame and power; it's the possibility that they will influence others that gets their engine running.

6. Power Motivation.
The type of person who's motivated by power has a strong need to be in control. They may like to delegate; they may not. They may want to influence others; they may not. There is, hopefully, a second motivation that fuels the intention, or it could end up not so good. It can be assumed that dictators are motivated by power. However, any President would have to have some of this motivation, but look to the why for the intention. We need people to be motivated by power, as they are not afraid to get out front.

7. Purpose Motivation.
Many have called this the "Rolls Royce" of motivators, because it goes to the very heart of why we all do what we do. People with purpose motivation are looking for a deep, meaningful experience in all they do and use words like *calling* or *purpose* when they describe what they do. I believe everyone has a purpose; they just haven't discovered it yet. Have you heard the cliché, "Once you find your purpose, you will never work another day in your life?" Your purpose is larger than you. It's a confidence that every day you are on this earth you are here for a reason. Those motivated by purpose (pastors, missionaries, doctors, singers) will speak with assurance. They know in their hearts they're doing what they're supposed to be doing with their lives.

Once you identify what motivates you, you can figure out what your true passions are and make a plan for pursuing them.

Are You Living the Right Dream?
I had it all. An enviable position with a company on the rise. A healthy six-figure income. I was rubbing shoulders with important

My Life Begins Next Monday...

people, enjoying all manner of perks, including a free trip to the Super Bowl and golfing on some of the best golf courses in the US. What more could I want? Especially considering all I had gone through to get where I was. I was at the top and climbing ever higher.

I had a dream job but wasn't living my dream.

The problem? I had a dream job but wasn't living my dream. My dream was to be a motivational speaker. I wanted to own my own business and spend my days influencing others. Instead, I was climbing a corporate ladder just like everyone else, for the money, the title, the security, the bigger house, the toys, the rings, the watches, the ego stuff society uses as a measuring stick to prove who is successful and who is not.

But, the higher I climbed on the ladder, the scarier it got to leap off. I don't want to say I built my ladder on the wrong building. I didn't make the wrong choice at the time. I just knew someday I'd use that same ladder to jump to another, better building. I knew deep down it wasn't my ultimate destination.

Maybe you can relate. Do any of these statements ring true with you?

> *I wish I were doing something else.*
> *I want to start my own business.*
> *This isn't how I want to spend my life.*
> *I wish I had balance in my life.*
> *There has got to be more than this.*

Are you in a dead-end job, one that won't lead to your dreams? Is it time for you to jump off that ladder you've been climbing and land on a different building altogether?

Many of us start the search for our life's passion from a place of unhappiness. We're so unhappy we say to ourselves, *"There's got to be more to life than this."* So, we go looking for something else. But many of us don't know how to find our passion in life. We start the search and have no idea what we're looking for, never mind how to find it.

You Have to Love What You Do
This is a good time for some clarification. There is a difference between what you're good at and what you love to do.

Just because you're good at something doesn't mean that's what you're destined to do with your life. You've got to be good at it *and* love it! Your sweet spot is where your talents and passion meet, not just where your skills lie. In Scott Fay's book *Discovering Your Sweet Spot* he says, "When you live in your sweet spot, you get results with very little effort."

One of the best ways to find your passion is to assess your strengths and talents. Why? When you can't/haven't identified your strengths and talents, you will work toward your goals inefficiently (if you work toward them at all). You'll put your thoughts, actions, and precious energy into the wrong things.

Assessing your strengths and talents allows you to use your time effectively, so you reach your goals sooner. And, you'll be happier doing it.

You see, when you don't like to do something—even if it comes easily to you—you're not going to perform at your peak. It can be draining mentally and physically. And, it depletes your "happiness quotient." Hence, it's not a strength. It's little more than a skill and, if you have to do it too often, it can become a weakness.

This is why, for our purposes, *a strength must not only be something you're good at, but something you enjoy doing.* A strength is something you could do over and over and over again and still perform at a high level. This is because you *enjoy* what you're doing.

The one thing I always fell back on was my work ethic. I was taught was to work hard. So I did. Then, after many years of reading and studying people like Tony Robbins, Brian Tracy, John C. Maxwell, and Dr. Bruce Schneider, I became obsessed with understanding *how* people are motivated and *why* they are better at some things than others, and what *working smarter not harder* meant.

As a senior in high school, I worked two jobs. At Burger King,

My Life Begins Next Monday...

I was known as the Drive-Thru Queen. I was great at my job, and I loved it. I had the Motivation to succeed, to achieve, to be the best, and I didn't let anything stand in my way. I might have had no friends (and no idea how to develop relationships), but I had my work ethic.

At 21, I put in long hours selling vacuum cleaners and encyclopedias, knocking on more doors and making more calls than anyone else. When I began selling for a cosmetics company, I was the top recruiter in Nebraska one year in my early twenties. But I still had no clue as to what my talent was. In spite of myself, I struggled to become successful over the years.

Now I know it's because I never tapped into the essence of what I was good at. I didn't discover this until later in my career.

I was good at connecting with people. I had a sense of humor. I had a natural talent for speaking in front of people. If someone had helped me see how my strengths and natural talent contributed to my success, I would have been successful much sooner—and I would have written this book (and others) years ago!

An Example of Loving What You Do
Let's say you have a child who's a talented gymnast. The coach says: "She could be a gold-medal Olympian if she trained six to eight hours a day, four to six times a week, over the next four years."

You ask your child if she wants to train for a shot at the Olympics, explaining to her in detail what it's going to entail. You say to her, "I'm not going to hound you to get up at 5:00 a.m. every morning to train before school, and keep up with your homework, and get you back to the gym for more training in the evenings."

You commit to playing chauffeur to and from her practices, and supporting her emotionally and financially, but you tell her, "You're going to have to take the lead. That means keeping your grades up, getting yourself up and out the door on time, and giving it your all at practice."

She agrees and follows through on everything.

She does this because she's passionate about gymnastics and the possibility of performing at the Olympics. Hence, she doesn't procrastinate; she sacrifices; and she engages in the activity even when she doesn't have to.

You don't have to force her out of bed in the mornings because she looks forward to practice. She keeps her grades up, because she knows that, if she starts to do poorly in school, she'll have to drop gymnastics (i.e., she sacrifices hours with friends to get her schoolwork done). She even practices "for free," with no one forcing her, on the day or two she's not officially training.

The moral of the story? When you *know* what you're put here to do (what your purpose in life is), bad habits like procrastination disappear. This is because you're in love; you're passionate about what you're doing. Then, you're more successful, because it's not a chore; you pour in the hours. You're also much happier; no one has to "push" you to perform. You want to perform!

Your success gives you more Confidence, which leads to more opportunities and more success, because you operate from a place of *"I can,"* instead of *"I can't,"* or *"What if,"* or *"Maybe I shouldn't."*

And this is what tapping into your strengths—and spending the majority of your time working in this zone—can do for you.

I've seen it time and time and time again in my success coaching business. Once I show my clients how to tap into their strengths, a whole new world opens up for them. This is the power—and reward—of tapping into your strengths to find your passion.

Now imagine how much different your life would be if you learned how to find your passion—and got to wake up every day and spend your energies doing what you love. What do you think you could achieve?

When Fear Blocks Your Path
If you've never taken the time to assess your strengths and talents, you're not alone. You would be surprised how many people don't do this. Why? Maybe it's fear: fear of failure, fear of the unknown, fear of the responsibility that comes with knowing what you love and are truly good at in life.

Fear is probably the biggest reason people waste their energy on their weaknesses. Many of my clients initially come to me desperately unhappy. They may have the trappings of success—a good job, a lucrative salary, on a high-flying success track—but inside they're miserable.

And it's because they're afraid of making a change. Fear keeps many locked into utilizing 75 percent of their energy on their weaknesses—instead of their strengths—because they're afraid to make a change. Fear is a powerful emotion that keeps many of us stuck at the starting gate.

Sometimes fear takes the form of low self-esteem. For example, you may talk yourself out of starting that bakery—which is something you've always wanted to do—because you don't feel you're smart enough about business.

Sometimes fear looks like lack of family support. Unfortunately, those who love us the most can often be the biggest barriers, not only finding our purpose in life, but doing something about it once we do.

For example, your brother may say, "You'd be crazy to give up your great job as a tax attorney to start a landscape architect business. I know you've always loved doing the outdoor thing, but making a business out of it? Come on, don't kid yourself."

These are just two examples. There are, of course, many others that put roadblocks in your way when you're learning how to find your passion in life—and desperately want to do something about it.

Sure, there's a lot to lose. Nothing good in life comes without a price. Without risk, there's no reward. We know these things.

A Simple Talent Detection Exercise
What if I told you I have a simple test you can take that will help you shave years off the road to success? You'd be all in, right?

This test will help you recognize—and tap into—those things you're naturally good at that can be developed into strengths. When you develop your natural talents and then marry them with your honed strengths, the possibilities are truly endless, both personally and professionally.

Here is a simple four-step talent detection exercise that will help you learn how to find your passion—and live the life you were truly meant to live.

Step 1: List All the Things You Think You're Good At. These would consist of things that come naturally to you (completing crossword puzzles, playing football, knitting, cooking, etc.).

Step 2: List Things Others Have Told You You're Good At. It can be difficult to do a true self-analysis like this; sometimes there are blind spots we just can't see. So list all the things others have told you you're good at—even if you don't think it's true. If possible, ask some friends or family members who know you well what they think you're good at. This can help to flesh out your "talent profile."

Step 3: Write Down Things You Like to Do. This isn't the same as Step 1. Sometimes there are things you like to do, but aren't good at, and vice versa. It's important to write these down.

Step 4: Rate Your Talents. On a scale of 1 to 10, rate how happy are you when you engage in a particular talent (1 = unhappy, and 10 = extremely happy). For example, if you have a talent for singing, but don't like to do it, then you might give this activity a 1 or 2. Once you do this, you'll gain some really good insight into exactly what your talents are.

The foundational reason for identifying your talents is so you can run your life more efficiently—in every area. You can use this knowledge to identify career and life options that add to your happiness, putting you light years ahead in every realm (career, personal relationships, etc.). Somewhere in here are the seeds to discovering what your passion and purpose in life are.

As a success coach, many successful (by society's standards) individuals have come to me very confused. They're asking the same questions so many of us ask at one time or another. The questions usually go something like this:

> *What is my life's purpose?*
> *How do I find my passion in life?*
> *What is my calling in life?*

I believe every single person already knows his/her passion—whether consciously or subconsciously. Some of us have to dig deeper than others to find it but, like DNA, it's such an integral part of who we are that it's never "missing." Where the real work comes in is what to do once we acknowledge what our purpose in life is.

Utilizing Your Strengths in the Business World
Knowing what you're good at (and what you like to do) will help you succeed in your career like never before. The 75/25 rule applies here as well.

> *Knowing what you're good at (and what you like to do) will help you succeed in your career like never before.*

In the corporate world, we get told what our responsibilities are, what the expectations are, and how we're supposed to do something. So, the talents and strengths that helped us get the position don't ever get used or honed. We get trained to go for the carrot, and our development goes to the wayside. We even start doing things we despise, tasks that drain the life out of us.

So, if you are part of an online PR business, for example, and everyone says you have to be active on social media, but you hate social media, how happy do you think you're going to be engaging in it?

Not only will you be unhappy, the return on your efforts won't be nearly what they would be if you enjoyed this activity. So, does this mean you should give up on social media? No. And that's the point of using the 75/25 rule.

You figure out what your strengths are so you can focus on them and find other ways to get done what you're not good at and/or don't enjoy doing.

For example, in this case, you might outsource your social media marketing to another team member or ask if an assistant will do it or even a friend for a $10 lunch card every week. It keeps your business front and center and leaves you to focus on what you enjoy most—interacting with your PR clients and finding different stories to pitch to the media to get them that all-important coverage.

One Entrepreneur's Success Story
Richard Leider, a leading authority and author of numerous books on how to find your purpose in life, wrote in *The Power of Purpose*:

> *If our purpose is genuine enough, it involves us deeply and orders all areas of our life. We begin to eliminate what is irrelevant and what is so much clutter. A simplification takes place, and we achieve a clarity as to what we're about. We don't need to pretend to be what we're not. What is of real importance stands out more clearly.*

Over the years, I have heard a lot of stories from those who take this advice to heart. One of my favorite examples is of an entrepreneur who owned a successful real estate business. Though she loved her profession, it wasn't her burning desire. What she really wanted to do was write; she'd known that since she was a small child. She also loved the ocean (and always had) and wanted to live where she could see it day in and day out. Her third goal was to travel.

However, everything she was doing in life was taking her away from her real passions. For one thing, she lived in a land-locked, cosmopolitan city with no ocean nearby. She also owned investment properties, which left her with no time to escape to the water and write, let alone travel for months at a time.

One day she actually sat down and wrote out her life plan. Upon seeing in black and white that she was working against herself on almost every level, she decided to make some drastic changes.

She sold her real estate holdings, started an online business that gave her the flexibility to work from anywhere, and settled on a small Caribbean island where she wrote every day.

Now, this didn't happen overnight, and she lived a "lower standard of living" than she had before. While her friends and family thought she'd lost her mind on some level, she'd never been happier. As a side bonus, she also lost 30 pounds (without really trying) and felt more content.

One big drawback of not "living your life on purpose" is stress. It's a silent killer. It's a major contributing factor—directly and/or indirectly—to a whole host of diseases, e.g., coronary artery disease, cancer, respiratory disorders, cirrhosis of the liver and suicide (the sixth leading cause of death in the U.S.).

This entrepreneur not only asked the question, "What is my purpose in life?" she answered it and took definitive action. This is what Leider meant when he said when you know your purpose—*a simplification takes place… what is of real importance stands out more clearly.*

You, Too, Can Achieve Your Dreams
I can confidently tell you: success also becomes that much more likely—because you're fueled by your very spirit, your heart, your soul, your being. Because of this, you have the energy you need to do what you may have thought was impossible before.

So, spend some time digging inside to find your purpose in life—and get busy pursuing it. It's a choice you'll never regret.

You see, only when you know yourself—inside and out—can you not only find your passion, but you'll have the courage to act upon it, and lead others to reach their full potential. It starts with your understanding of what truly motivates you.

THE APPLICATION BLUEPRINT

So, never fear that you're someone without a passion. You're not. Everyone has one. Are you ready for some more simple exercises to help you discover your passion?

1. Fill in the Blanks.

If money were no object, I'd _____.
As a child, I wanted to be a _____.
In my spare time, I like to _____.
If I could start my career all over, I'd _____.

Now, add the words "and then" to the end of each sentence. "If money were no object, <u>I'd quit my day job</u> and then <u>I'd open my own Bed & Breakfast</u>.

_____
_____
_____
_____
_____
_____
_____
_____
_____
_____

For some of us, this simple exercise is too difficult because of the self-imposed limits we're holding on to (sometimes without even realizing it). Things like low self-esteem, fear of disapproval from those we love, etc.

My Life Begins Next Monday...

2. If #1 didn't work for you, try filling in the following blanks.

If I had no one but myself to consider, I'd _____.
If I knew my friends and family would approve, I'd _____.
If I could afford to hire an expert to help me, I'd _____.
If I was X years younger, I'd _____.

3. How about you? What motivates you? What do you want out of life? What wakes you up in the morning? Look back over your responses to each motivation. Which one stands out to you? What have you learned about yourself after doing this exercise?

_____
_____
_____
_____
_____
_____
_____
_____
_____
_____

My mantra is this: "When you marry your strengths with your talents, the possibilities truly are endless." Have you taken the time to identify your strengths and talents? I'll give you some helpful tips for doing that very thing in a bit, but first, go ahead and share them as you see them.

4. Now it's time to put pen to paper and make a list of all your fears—everything from the possibility of the disapproval of friends and family to your own insecurities to practical fears like "What if I can't support my family?"

_____
_____
_____
_____
_____
_____
_____
_____
_____
_____

5. Now, write down a "what's the worst that could happen?" statement. It's at this point that a light bulb usually goes off for many. They realize they can overcome a lot of their fears, but what many never confront is the "what's the worst that could happen?" part of the equation. Try it. Ask yourself what's the worst that could happen if you pursue your dream?

_____
_____
_____
_____
_____
_____
_____
_____
_____
_____

6. What are some weaknesses you've been spending too much time on in your business? How could you delegate those so that you can focus more of your time and energy on your strengths?

_____
_____
_____
_____
_____
_____
_____
_____
_____
_____

THE TAKEAWAY

What is one thing you can take away from this chapter and apply to your personal life?

_____
_____
_____

What is one thing you can take away from this chapter and apply to your business or career?

_____
_____
_____

What is one tangible, practical thing you can do today that will make a difference tomorrow?

_____
_____
_____

My Life Begins Next Monday...

The Box

*It's a box.
Yes, a cardboard box.
It's just a box.
But the possibilities are endless.

It's a ship to carry precious cargo.
It's a safe to hold your gold.
It's a drum to keep the beat.
It's just a box?
Aren't the possibilities endless?

It's your box.
Yes, your world is a box.
It's not just any box.
The possibilities are endless.

So take your box.
Carry your thoughts, your precious cargo.
Open the safe, the gold of your heart.
Beat your drum, and make music for others to hear.
It's your box.
The possibilities are endless.

But, sharing what is in the box
Is the key to making the possibilities endless.*

Chapter 5: Confidence

*Believe you can,
and you're halfway there.*

–Theodore Roosevelt

5

It's very difficult to build your Confidence when you're living in Survival or Denial. You may be doing a little task and feel accomplished for a moment (which is the pure essence of Survival, or we would fall into a deep depression). But, to truly build Confidence, you have to accept yourself, your situation, who you are in every way, and move forward from there.

Then, once we begin to acknowledge what motivates us, what we value, what revs our engine, what wakes us up in the morning and gets us excited to be on this planet, we can begin to build our Confidence. We can grow that sweet assurance in our minds and hearts that we deserve to live this life; we deserve to have happiness; we can accomplish what we put our mind to. We can do this!

The Confidence Stage is about learning to have a mindset that you can depend on *you*. That nobody is going to shake what you want to learn, what you have to offer, or have input on how you see and feel about yourself. One of the first things to learn is how to block out negative talk (and negative people, for that matter). If you let in negativity of any kind, if you let people say you can't do something, you're going to lose sight of who you want to become, of your goals. When we start to waver is when our Confidence starts to waver.

That's one thing people have always complimented me on: she's doing exactly what she said she was going to do. Confidence is a strong suit of mine; it can be one of yours too.

Fear Isn't Bad
What's the opposite of Confidence? Fear, right? Most of us think of fear as a bad thing. But, like every other human emotion, it's actually a necessary part of survival. In essence, fear is a protective emotion—nothing more, nothing less.

Let's look at fear, not as a red light, but as a yellow one, encouraging you to proceed with caution. The feelings of fear you experience as you think about pursuing your passion, or anything outside your comfort zone, are not there to stop you! They exist to encourage you to take a breath and *logically* (as opposed to fearfully) assess the pros and cons.

If you are doing something new, your inner critic's job is to protect you from failing by making you slow down and gather concrete facts, so you can move forward in a more confident manner. Yes, that's right. It's not so you can look back and think of all the things you have tried and failed, all the times you could have done better, all the people you hurt, or all the things you said you were going to do and didn't. It is there so, *moving forward*, your awareness of consequences is present. That's it. Once you acknowledge the consequences, you make a decision and move on. Confidence comes from action, no matter the result. So, acknowledge your inner critic; give thanks to it, knowing it's there to help *guide* you in the right direction.

Courage isn't the absence of fear. It's taking that first step in spite of fear, in the face of fear. If you wait for feelings of fear to dissipate before you make a move, you'll be waiting for the rest of your life. This is exactly why people get stuck where they're at and fail to move forward in Confidence.

Something Was Holding Me Back
Up until the day I decided to leave my corporate job, I had dreamt of writing this book, starting my own company, speaking, and inspiring millions! And I could've achieved that dream a lot sooner than I did, except for one small (big) problem.

I had defined myself as somebody who was *less than*.

Who will listen to me?

I would ask myself, "Who will listen to me? Why would they listen to me? I'm not smart." Oh, those awful voices we hear in our heads. I had defined myself as a high school dropout, even if I did go back and get my GED when I was 21, and who listens to high school dropouts?

I was not good enough, not smart enough, not capable enough, not worthy of people's respect. How many times have you thought that to yourself?

Confidence-building has to be intentional. Once I started writing the final version of this book, I was on a roll. Then...right about this chapter (kind of ironic), I hit a wall. The old fears crept back in. We were right on the edge of getting this to the publisher, and I got stuck.

I started thinking about the reaction of my friends, my family, strangers, and everyone I have told about this for the past twenty years. Like tear gas creeping under a doorway, silent but deadly, I was gripped by fear. I called Marla, my professional writing partner, and made excuses.

The bottom line? I was scared to death this was actually going to happen. It wasn't failure I was scared of; it was success.

I put everything down that had anything to do with the book and focused on every other part of my business. I dove headfirst into the Denial Stage. I had to live the Stages all over again.

Oh, the irony.

It wasn't until I accepted, wholeheartedly, that sharing these stages was about helping people, and it didn't matter how successful it became, that I was able to start the final editing. I told my ego, "Thank you for trying to protect me from what may or may not happen in the future, but I've got this."

Sticks and Stones May Break My Bones...
Sometimes we get the idea that we're not good enough from another person in our lives, often someone we're related to. Remember that old (ridiculous) jingle, "Sticks and stones may break my bones, but words will never hurt me!"

Who in the world made up that load of crap? Words hurt more than any sticks or stones, and the wounds take so, so much longer to heal.

Remember my story about my 10-year-old Cher-wanna-be self? How my mom effectively crushed my dreams in one fell swoop?

In my opinion, my mom was still living in Survival and Denial. She hadn't made it past that. She couldn't imagine a bright future for herself, let alone her daughter. She couldn't see beyond today. In my generous moments, I believe she was actually trying to protect me from disappointment and rejection. She was warning me that life was about surviving, not dreaming.

Unfortunately, her dire predictions for me came true—for quite a few years at least. Until I learned how to shed that curse of "You'll Never Be Somebody" and realized it was okay to dream.

My Confidence was built, for many years, out of a negative Motivation to prove to her that I could be somebody. I was either proving her right or proving her wrong. Proving I could have something and I was worth it. I may not have believed it deep down, but I took action.

So, whatever you use to get you moving forward out of Survival and Denial will build Confidence in the fact that you can take action. Acceptance will come as you are moving forward, and your Confidence will build.

Don't Read the Labels
In my career, I had taken many personality tests and loved them. They helped me with my awareness of how people saw me and what I needed to work on. The problem was my peers then had a label for me, especially if they did not have the same profile. Then, when I would grow or stretch myself to improve, I was held captive by that label. I wasn't allowed to become something different or better.

In the past few years, I have noticed so many people who are merely existing. They're not living fulfilled lives. But they have no idea how to break free.

I wanted to create a profile that focuses on our strengths and how we work, so we aren't worried about how to shed a label. We could connect with others based on how we work in any situation, not just a perception. When we build on strengths, our confidence multiplies exponentially. Be aware of weaknesses, but focus on strengths.

I want you to have confidence in who you really are, not in what some label says you are. There are many assessments available to give you insight into what your strengths are.

How to Gain Confidence
One of the things I learned early on, when I started leading people, is that everyone seeking my help has different reasons for not achieving their goals. Each reason (excuse) almost always stems from some form of self-doubt. Hence, many of the conversations I have, to this day, revolve around increasing a person's knowledge on how to gain

Confidence. They need to know how to break through their limiting beliefs, so that they can get on the road to living the life they really want.

Here are three things you can start doing—immediately:

1. Identify It. Dr. Phil is famous for saying, "You can't change what you don't acknowledge." The first exercise in learning how to gain Confidence is to get out a pad and pencil and write down what you're afraid of, the leading causes of your fears and insecurities.

For example, do you think you can't quit your high-paying job to start that business because everyone will think you're crazy? Do you think that, because you have no entrepreneurial experience, if it fails, you will be perceived as a failure?

Tip: while laptops and tablets and pads are great, there's something powerful in sitting down with good ol' pen and paper (this book!) and physically writing this information down. It's as if your fears flow through the pen onto the page—physically freeing you from their existence.

2. What's the Worst That Could Happen? We talked about this in the last chapter, but it bears repeating. I really want you to get this. One of the keys in learning how to gain Confidence is to think logically through the fear process. Using the scenario in #1 above, if you did quit your high-paying job to pursue a business you love, what's the worst thing that could happen if it failed?

Seriously, what is the very worst thing that could happen if you go after your dream and you fail? Write it down right now.

Ironically, what most realize when they answer this question is it's not nearly as bad as they thought.

3. Create a Plan. One of the oldest idioms in business is: "If you fail to plan, you plan to fail." This applies to life as well.

One of the best ways to face fear of failure is to plan for success. Overcoming fear gets you on the road to developing self-esteem and improving self-confidence.

Go ahead and start making a plan right now. What are some concrete steps you can take to get you moving forward toward your dream?

Once you learn how to gain Confidence, you move through life with a different view of the world. It doesn't mean you never experience self-doubt or have brushes with low self-esteem again. What it does mean is that you're better equipped to deal with them—and not let them keep you from pursuing your dreams.

Three Things You Can Do Right Now to Silence Your "Inner Critic"

Lacking self-confidence stems from a whole myriad of factors (how we were raised, how we look, how smart we are, etc.). Some of these things we can control; others we can't. A chronic lack of Confidence can be largely attributed to the voice in our heads—what psychologists frequently refer to as our inner critic.

In spite of this, we can learn how to become more confident. Many times all we have to do is learn how to turn off this voice—or at least quiet it.

But, before that, let's look at the toll this voice takes on our lives.

"I'm never going to get that promotion. Jane is way more qualified."

"You have to have the right connections to get appointed to that committee; there's no way I'll be seriously considered."

"I hate my hair; it looks like a disheveled mop. Man, I wish I had straight hair!"

For many, thoughts like these run through our heads on autopilot. Why aren't positive thoughts just as easy to come by? The simple fact is: many of us are so accustomed to thinking of ourselves as "less than" that we don't even stop to question why.

And, make no mistake, these thoughts have a profound effect on how we live our lives. If you believe Jane is more qualified than you for a promotion, you're unlikely to put forth the effort needed to get the promotion. After all, why bother? Jane *is* more qualified than little ol' you.

And this is why it's necessary to learn how to become more confident. To this end, there are three easy things you can do—right away—to silence the inner critic in your head and get on the road to becoming more confident.

1. Acknowledge the Thought: When negative thoughts rear their unproductive heads, stop and take a moment to recognize this. *"I just told myself I'm not connected enough to get that committee appointment."*

The reason this is important: you can't change what you don't acknowledge.

2. Combat It with Positivity: The minute you recognize the thought, come up with a positive counter to it. *"I was tops in sales, and my boss gave me a sterling review last quarter. I could ask her for a recommendation."*

One of the quickest ways to learn how to become more confident is to replace the critical thought with a positive one. This is called Auto Suggestion. If you want to really learn about this subject, Napoleon Hill writes about Auto Suggestion in his book, *Think and Grow Rich.* I read this book at least once a year.

3. Write It Down: If you keep a journal, skim back through it for a few minutes. Are you surprised by how often you tell yourself negative things? This leads to low self-esteem, which leads to dream-snatching behavior. There's nothing like seeing it in black and white to start actively combating it all the time.

Take a few minutes to write down some negative thoughts you often have. Then strike a line through each one, and write down a positive thought to take its place.

Learning how to become more confident takes practice—like any skill worth learning—but it's critical to having the courage to living the full, rich life you deserve.

Embracing Your Inner Critic in Three Simple Steps
When most professionals talk about "the inner critic," the advice focuses on silencing it or getting rid of it. As a success coach, I've taught hundreds how to do this. However, for some, this can be counterproductive.

Why? It's like telling someone not to think about pink elephants. And we all know where that leads.

Here are three things you can do to embrace your inner critic and learn how to be more confident because of it. It's just a different way of solving the same lack of self-confidence problem.

1. What's It Really Saying to You: I heard someone once say (on Oprah) that all emotions are based on two things: love and fear. For example, low self-esteem is really just a "fear" that you're not good enough.

So the next time your inner critic says something like, "*You'll never get that promotion because you're not as qualified as Jane,*" don't internalize it that way. Stop and examine the underlying emotion. In this case, it's really just a fear that you're not qualified for the position at hand. This fear can be real or imagined, which brings us to the next step.

2. Is the Message Justified? Ask yourself, "*Is what the inner critic is telling me based on fear or reality?*" Many of us repeat negative messages to ourselves out of sheer habit. We never stop to examine if the message is really justified.

One of the first lessons in learning how to be more confident is having the "cojones," if you will, to question the situation at hand. If you suffer from low self-esteem and a lack of Confidence, this may seem strange, even scary, at first. With practice, it can become second nature.

When asking if the message is justified, approach your answer in a purely analytical way—using facts, not feelings. This brings us to the final step.

3. Make a List: Put pen to paper so you can see in black and white what the facts are. Using the example above about the promotion, once you start to list your accomplishments, you may realize, "I served on two committees in the last 12 months; my team met and exceeded its sales quota by 12%; and I've already been cross-trained on the new data system the company will be rolling out next quarter."

Learning how to become confident requires mental training, similar to running a marathon.

Learning how to become more confident requires mental training, similar to running a marathon. And the training starts with allowing yourself to embrace your inner critic. Then, instead of getting into a battle with yourself, you "consult" with a "friend" (that inner critic that lives in your head).

See the difference? It's a big one.

Overcoming Limitations
Almost every human being has a dream, a burning passion they'd pursue if they weren't held back by what I call "life limitations." Life limitations can manifest themselves as lack of money, education, or experience. What holds most of us back though aren't these things—at least not wholly.

One of the main stumbling blocks for many when it comes to pursuing their passion is a lack of Confidence. Let's examine the first step in learning how to become more confident so you can pursue your real passion(s) in life.

All of us are born the same way—naked—without preconceived notions of who we are or should be, without judgment attached to what we did or didn't do. Why is this important? Because the first step in learning how to be more confident is to realize that lacking Confidence is a learned trait.

And, if it's learned, it can be unlearned.

We all spring from the womb naked of everything. As we grow, influences start to build up and can chip away at who we are, think we are, want to be, think we want to be, etc.

The kids pick on you in school for being too skinny; this chips away at your Confidence.

You don't get into the college of your choice; your inner critic whispers you're not smart enough.

You get overlooked at work for a promotion; this lowers your self-esteem.

See how all of life's happenings can paint a picture—one that reinforces the idea that you're not good enough? This leads to a lack of self-confidence.

Even though the "bad" things that happen in life are simply

opportunities to learn, as human beings, we tend to ingest them as life lessons reinforcing the fact that we're somehow failures. But what if you could go back to being as free from these types of judgments and limitations as the day you were born? What would you do differently as you grew, as life threw challenges and (perceived) limitations your way?

I believe all of us are born with Confidence. And it's either reinforced or gets stripped away based on our socialization. Some of this, unfortunately, we have no control over. For example, how our parents encourage/discourage us as we grow. But the wonderful thing about being an adult is that you get to choose your destiny.

So, remember, the Confidence you need to pursue your passion—whatever it is—is already within you.

> *So, remember, the Confidence you need to pursue your passion—whatever it is— is already within you.*

You just may have to dig a bit deeper than others to tap into it. Once found, though, the successive steps you need to take on your journey to Confidence will be that much easier.

A Roadmap for Increasing Your Confidence
We talked about strengths and talents in the previous chapter, and we'll continue that discussion now, because utilizing them effectively is key to increasing Confidence. As a success coach, one of the things I've found over the years is that those who struggle with becoming more confident often do so because they don't know what their talents and strengths are—or how to use them in their quest for success.

It's one of the reasons I developed www.StrongSuccessAcademy.com™, a place to create your individualized self-development plan that helps you identify your strengths and talents, so you can harness them and achieve your goals.

I see at least three advantages to identifying your strengths and talents.

1. When you know your strengths—and work with them—you're automatically more productive and energetic, which brings us to reason number two.

2. You waste less time because you're not working in your weak zone, but in your strength zone; and finally...

3. You learn how to harness the power of your talents and marry them with your strengths—which produces incredible results.

When you marry your innate strengths with your honed talents, you reach your highest potential. As you learn about yourself (your strengths, your weaknesses, your talents), you gain Confidence in your abilities and how to effectively fortify your weaknesses.

This is the kind of data elite athletes like Tiger Woods use to improve their performance. They are taught very early in their careers to "play to their strengths," a lesson most of us never learn.

Many never reach their potential because they've never been given a roadmap on how to get there. Hence, they spend almost their entire lives working beneath their capacity, or working more with their weaknesses than with their strengths and talents.

But, once you know what the keys are to becoming more confident, it's like a whole new world opens up—a world of endless possibilities for you.

Taking a Leap and Starting My Own Business

I took a deep breath and jumped. I left my more-than-comfortable, well-paying job and ventured out on my own. I had the money. I had a plan. But I had no guarantee it would work. I had my husband's support (and he agreed we'd use our 401K to get my business off the ground). If we didn't try now, when would we do it? I had rationalized in my head that the time was right. I was young and could get another job if I needed to. But, if I waited 10 years, it might be too late. If I wasn't willing to go all in on myself, who would be?

For years, I had been waiting to live my dream; yet I was too focused on all the reasons I shouldn't follow my passion, instead of why I should. It was as if I had an epiphany. I realized I had to *choose* to move forward and design the life I wanted, not wait for the time to be right for it to magically materialize.

By the end of that week, Strong Organization, LLC had been formed. Deep down in my gut I *knew* it was the right move, that the time had come for me to chart my own path.

I was confident I could do it, and yet still scared to death. I decided that, come hell or high water, I would stick it out for a year. No matter how hard things got, I wouldn't even entertain the idea of throwing in the towel until the one-year mark.

That kept me going more days than I can count.

Let's Talk About Failure
I don't know the exact numbers, but a huge amount of new business start-ups fail in the first year. 25% fail in year one, 36% fail in year two, 44% fail in year three.

That's not very encouraging, is it?

But what if we look at the flipside of that? After one year, 75% of new businesses still have their doors open. After two years, 64% are still in business. After three years, 56% are still going strong. Instead of looking at people who fail, let's look at the people who made it. What did they do right?

First of all, they're willing to suspend instant gratification. They're not expecting everything to go well from day one. They decide to work hard no matter what.

I promised myself I would not make a rash decision, that I wouldn't quit based on emotions. I cried almost every single day for the first six months I was out on my own.

I was having a blast, but I was so busy. And I made a lot of mistakes. Looking back now, I see that my business was a result of operating out of fear. But I committed not to quit. And I didn't.

That's the second characteristic of a business that lasts. No quitting. I had a mentor say to me once, "I'm an entrepreneur now. I get to pick the 80 hours of the week I work." You've got to keep that dream in mind. Always. It's going to be hard. Don't give up.

Successful business-owners focus. Instead of trying to serve everybody and chasing after a million different things, they choose one thing to focus on. They do one thing well, not a bunch of things kind-of well. They fight the urge to be multi-passion-istas.

And last, but not least, they don't let their ego get in the way. They're not afraid to do the dirty work, and they learn from their mistakes. They go from "being in love" with their potential, as Mark LeBlanc, the author of *Growing Your Business,* says to taking steps to reach it.

Let's Move Forward with Confidence!
Here's the thing. We're afraid to take a risk, to take a step into the unknown, because what if we fail? What will people say?

But, you know what, friend? In reality, people aren't sitting around talking about you and whether or not you achieved your dream. They're not sitting around talking about me either. They just aren't. People are worried about themselves, not you or me.

In reality, people will be inspired by you. They'll want to follow your lead. Even if you "fail," they'll admire you for trying. You'll find people who want to encourage you, and they will.

Be confident in yourself, in your abilities. Be confident you have what it takes to pursue your dreams. Be confident you were created for a purpose, and your life can be anything you make it! The four D's are: Define It, Decide It, Design It, and Do It. You can do this, friend!

THE APPLICATION BLUEPRINT

1. Has someone in your life, someone close to you, stepped on your dreams and crushed them? Who was it, and how did it make you feel?

_____
_____
_____
_____
_____

Have you heard the phrase, "Hurt people hurt people"? In my case, my mom was dealing with her own stuff, so she was quick to snuff out my dreams. Sometimes people say cruel things to us because they've been hurt by others first.

Forgiving that person and moving on can be a powerful step in the direction toward pursuing your dreams. You can forgive that person face-to-face, through a letter or e-mail, or you can just declare in your heart that you have forgiven them and promise yourself not to dwell any longer on the hurt they've caused you.

We'll talk more about forgiveness in Chapter 7.

2. What are some labels you have been given (and believed) over the years?

_____
_____
_____
_____
_____

3. How might you go about shedding some of those labels? How will that make you feel? How will it change your life?

_____
_____
_____
_____
_____

4. What are you afraid of right now? No fear is too big or too silly. Write it all down.

_____
_____
_____
_____
_____

5. List your accomplishments here:

_____
_____
_____
_____
_____

6. What is one brave, bold, confident thing you can do TODAY?

_____
_____
_____
_____
_____

THE TAKEAWAY

What is one thing you can take away from this chapter and apply to your personal life?
_____
_____
_____

What is one thing you can take away from this chapter and apply to your business or career?
_____
_____
_____

What is one tangible, practical thing you can do today that will make a difference tomorrow?
_____
_____
_____

My Life Begins Next Monday...

Journey to Believe

It's not my head that needs to understand.
It's my heart that cries to be heard.
I am scared.

What will they say?
My mouth opens and no sound comes out.
I am scared.

I need you to believe in me
Before I can reach for the stars.
I am scared.

One step, one sound, one smile
That will give me hope and belief.
I can do this.

Somewhere between here and there
My story can be told.
I can do this.

Rise and shine; that is what I can do
It's not how fast I go.
I can do this.

Listen and be confident and know that
My story, my soul, my spirit
Has purpose.

Shari Strong

Every moment of my life,
Because of my purpose,
I can be sure.

I am scared.
I can do this.
I have purpose.
I can be sure.

Chapter 6: Connection

*A dream you dream alone
is only a dream.
A dream you dream together is reality.*

−John Lennon

6

Years ago, Nicholas Negroponte, the founder of the MIT Media Lab, made predictions of innovation that many people laughed at.

Funny, they aren't laughing now.

Nicholas has a brilliant mind that is able to understand the needs of man and our evolution and brings solutions to those needs. In one of his most recent speeches at a TED Conference, he stated, "…the challenge in the next thirty years will be to connect the next billion people to each other. The first billion, the low hanging fruit, was easy."

When I heard him speaking about connecting a billion people, the hairs on my arms stood up. My heart started to race. "That's it! That is exactly what I want to do!"

Now, how he does it and how I do it and the reasons *why* may be different, but the realization that no man is an island is the same. We need people in our lives. We just do. It's all fine and good to accept yourself and be confident in who you are, survive this life, understand Denial, dream and grow, but… if you're doing it all alone… that is neither fine *nor* good.

> *The temptation when you've been hurt/betrayed by people is to put up walls, to keep people out, and decide to face the world on your own.*

The temptation when you've been hurt/betrayed by people is to put up walls, to keep people out, and decide to face the world on your own. We think that is the easy way. When you have been very successful based on hard work, or even luck, it's easy to say you don't need others.

But here is the truth: we were made for community. We need each other. Life just works better when we live it together. And when it comes to achieving our goals and living our dreams, we need other people too. If our dreams aren't bigger than ourselves, then they're not big enough.

John Maxwell, one of my mentors, is a noted international speaker, author, and personal development leader. One of his most powerful books (and he has many) is *The 21 Irrefutable Laws of Leadership*.

Of those 21 laws, perhaps the most important, when it comes to self-improvement and personal development, is "The Law of Connection." Its foundation is the belief that, in order for leaders to be effective, they must connect with people. And, in order for us to lead others, we must first lead ourselves.

First, before we can bring others into our world or lead ourselves, we have to know ourselves and be at peace with who we are. We have to connect with ourselves, so to speak, before we can truly connect with others in meaningful ways.

In the end, it's all about 1.) Self-awareness (connecting with yourself). 2.) People. 3.) The ability to connect the two.

Let's break this down.

Connecting with Yourself
So many people have a difficult time connecting with others and maintaining relationships that last longer than a few months. Have you ever heard *you have friends for a reason or a season*? This may be true but, in either case, your ability to connect with others will determine if the reason turns into a season and how long the season will last.

There's a verse in the Bible that says, "Love your neighbor as you love yourself." We all heartily agree that loving others is important, but many of us don't realize you have to love yourself first. Not in a self-centered, prideful way, but in a healthy, nurturing way.

How do you honestly feel about yourself? Here's the thing. If we're in the Survival or Denial Stages, if we haven't accepted who we are and don't understand our own Motivations, it's going to be pretty tough to connect with others. We have to connect with ourselves first.

My Life Begins Next Monday...

My family was always moving when I was growing up. We'd get settled in one place, then have to pack everything up and move to a brand new one. I didn't really mind it but, looking back, it sure wasn't easy. It's hard to keep starting over, to not know anyone, to always have to make new friends. And I wasn't really good at that anyway.

All this disconnecting caught up with me my junior year in high school. At a crucial time in a young girl's life when she really needs to feel like she belongs and has people who care about her, I felt like I had no one.

I had low self-awareness, low self-esteem, and very few people skills or communication skills. I learned early on that I had a great work ethic (I made a few hundred dollars a week), but working hard was all I was really good at. I was severely lacking in social skills.

It was during this vulnerable time that I met Richard. I was 16; he was 22. We worked at the same restaurant. He had two beautiful little blond-haired, blue-eyed boys (his wife had left him) and needed a babysitter a couple times. I took the job, and it led to a relationship with Richard. I didn't have any other friends. He was my only one.

A few years later, when Richard and the boys went back to Texas without me, I was in the same boat as when we met, but worse. I still hadn't learned communication skills or how to listen to others. My belly was growing; the three people who loved me were gone; I was alone; and my spirit was lost.

One sad byproduct of living in the Survival Stage is, when we get hurt by people, the walls go up, and that stop us from connecting with people at an intimate level. I felt hurt by my mother. Richard had hurt me physically and mentally. I didn't have any true friends because of moving so often, so I was determined to never have to depend on anyone else ever again. All I needed was myself. I was the only one I could count on. My ability to connect was null and void. Why would I need to connect with anyone if I wasn't going to depend on anyone?

This is a classic Survival Stage thought process. I have worked with many people over the years in sales, MLM companies, and networking groups who developed these habits while in the Survival or Denial Stages. If we're not intentional about changing our actions, we will tend to fall back to those same habits any time we're under stress or in unfamiliar situations.

We set our self-esteem level while living in any stage, but the Survival Stage creates the foundation. The foundation is what we will go back to when we feel threatened or out of our comfort zone. This often stops us from connecting with people who are in our lives now. How long or how often we fall back will determine our identity in the future. It will determine whether we reach our potential and develop our God-given abilities, or embrace a victim mentality and camp out here forever.

Raising our awareness of our identity will help us accept responsibility when we make mistakes in the future, accept others more easily, and understand multiple perspectives. The bottom line when it comes to connecting with ourselves? Understanding we are right where we are supposed to be. Tomorrow we will be too.

So, what can you do today to be a better you?

> *We are right where we are supposed to be. Tomorrow we will be too. So, what can you do today to be a better you?*

Connect with the Moment
In the past five years, I started going to plays for the first time in my life—Wicked, The Lion King, Shrek. Now I can't get enough. When you're sitting watching a production, you have to let yourself go; you have to be in the moment. You have to enjoy it and be intentional in it, or you're not going to get anything out of it. When you're able to be all there, fully present, to soak it all in, your experience is rich and full.

A few years ago, I had a conversation with a former co-worker. She was a VP, and I had watched her move up the corporate ladder. She is way more analytical than I am, and she had trouble understanding why people would get emotional over things she saw as merely part of one job or another. While everyone liked her, many would make comments about not having a connection with her. People weren't sure they could trust her.

She and I got to talking about Broadway plays, and she shared that she didn't like them. She said she just "doesn't get them." She was open to trying though, so we went to see The Lion King together, but that's where it ended. She still didn't get it.

Now, I'm not saying everybody has to go to plays—or even like plays. As the old adage says, one will either love the opera or hate it. But, just like her inability to connect with something that "wasn't her thing," she had a hard time connecting with people or experiences that weren't like her or things she liked. While we may not like everything or everybody we meet, that doesn't mean we can't connect with the moment or them. It's just going to take a bit of extra effort, that's all.

Have you ever met someone and said to yourself, "I can't connect with this guy." Or maybe at work you think, "I have a hard time connecting with my boss."

Here's the point. It's a choice. It's a matter of how much time and effort you are willing to give to make that connection. The ability to connect with people—all kinds of people—is an ability you need if you're going to live your dreams.

You don't get what you want; you get who you are.

You don't get what you want; you get who you are.

What does that mean? So many times we say we want this, we want that, we want more than we have: in relationships, financially, our careers, our hobbies, etc. I believe this means we have exactly what we believe we are worth.

This applies to teams in the workplace as well. Managers who say, "I wish I had a better team," won't get one. They have who they are, not what they want.

The Connection Stage is all about choice. Sometimes Connection is scary. To have true Connection with someone, you have to be vulnerable. Generally, our society does not encourage us to be vulnerable, so we are not good at it. We'd rather be in control. We'd rather avoid the possibility of getting hurt. We put up walls to keep that from happening. But guess what? It's hard to connect with someone when there's a wall between the two of you. Own that. Don't go back to the Survival Stage or the Denial Stage. Do the hard, rewarding work of the Connection Stage.

Over my career, there was a theme running through the feedback I got from a number of different bosses: "your people love you, but your peers don't."

It took me a long time to understand why. I didn't know how to connect with them. I was great with leading people who needed my expertise but not so hot with connecting with people who didn't. It wasn't out of arrogance; it was out of having some success with developing people. I would ask myself, "Why in the world would they not want to know what I am doing?"

I can honestly say that every team I have had the pleasure of building was successful. A VP of Sales once gave me one of the best compliments I had ever received, "Shari, everything you touch turns to gold."

Yet, I had a hard time connecting with peers.

It wasn't until a my late 30's that I started to understand Zig Ziglar's saying, "People don't care how much you know, until they know how much you care."

I always thought that was for the people I led. Guess what? It was for my peers too. I had to learn to back off, ask those questions, be interested in them, control my energy, and understand that there was more than one way to build successful teams.

Once the switch got flipped, everything changed.

Why You Need to Develop Soft Skills
Knowing how to make Connections with others is more important now than ever before. In the past, when looking for employees, most employers focused on hard skills. In other words, does the prospective

employee have the necessary training to do this particular job?

While these skills are still a big part of the hiring/promotional process, the birth of the global economy gives equal (and sometimes, greater) weight to soft skills.

What are soft skills? Soft skills are a set of interpersonal traits that make a person a good employee. A person with an enviable set of soft skills is: optimistic, empathetic, well-mannered, sociable, responsible, inspirational, encouraging, open to change, etc.

Nowadays, business is done worldwide. Executives are required to interact with people and cultures they may have never encountered before. Hence, it's not enough to "be nice." You have to make a Connection.

People do business with those they: 1.) know 2.) like and 3.) trust. You have to connect with them before any of this can take place. You may be thinking at this point, "I am not going into the corporate world, so what does this have to do with me?"

Are you a parent? Parents tend to focus on their kids playing an instrument, being the best at sports, getting great grades, but the teaching of communication has gone to the technical world. The use of laptops, iPhones, iPads, virtual games, spell check, Wikipedia, etc, has left our younger generation in a dangerous crossroads of learning. I do not advocate getting rid of any of the devices, but I do feel that courses on human behavior, how to interact, and the ability to think things through from another's perspective will go to the wayside if we do not make them a priority. In the end, people use the items listed, people develop them, and this world is all about people.

Here are some of the skills necessary to succeed in today's global culture—and in your local community, church, networking group, or book club:

Communication Skills. Nothing productive can take place until you can effectively communicate with many different personality styles and educational levels. And, again, this requires much more than just being nice. Connecting is more skill than natural talent, and anyone can develop this.

Influence. Once you have effective communication, you have the person's attention and are well on your way to gaining their trust. Then, you can begin to influence the relationship. We all get to decide, in any moment, our attitude and focus, which will influence the depth of the Connection. Influence does not mean power. It can lead to power, but the results will come from your level of influence, not your level of power.

Embrace and Perform as a Leader: Once you're recognized as a leader, the sky is the limit—if you know how to perform as one. We are all leaders. Mothers lead children. Fathers lead families. Managers lead teams or projects. Pastors lead churches. People lead committees, non-profits, networking groups. And, most importantly, you lead yourself.

Awareness of Purpose: True leaders know where they're going. It's one of the main reasons they can find a way to connect with—and influence—others to follow them.

Operating in a global economy calls on skills most middle managers either don't have, or that are severely underdeveloped. Parents have trouble connecting with their children because they are out of touch and haven't developed a Family Purpose or Goal or don't understand their child's purpose or goal.

What It Takes to Be an Effective Manager of Ourselves

Managers, in particular, face unique challenges in this day and age. Just like we are all leaders, we are all managers. The difference? Managers lead things or projects and leaders lead people. One way to look at the responsibilities of managers is as the "bridge over an entire organization." Why? Because they often have a hand in every corporate pie—from managing people and budgets to developing and overseeing operational processes and organizational objectives.

In a family, mothers and fathers have to know when to delegate and when to take control. Their ability to bridge the needs of each child with the needs of the family will reveal the level of Connection they have with each family member.

Here are some of the many challenges:

Managing the Culture:

Corporate: From handling the dissatisfaction of entry-level employees to reaching the objectives of senior-level management.

Family: Decisions on how many activities each child can participate in and still have a family focus.

Community: If you have neighbors you haven't spoken to in the last year, this is an example of the culture being spread around the world. Be intentional. The need to help each other, listen to each other, and acknowledge each other is greater than ever before and will continue to create a gap if we don't acknowledge the need for Connection.

Reconciling goals:

Corporate: These can sometimes be disparate objectives, e.g., increasing production while cutting staff overhead. Understanding the big picture at your business and learning skills to close those gaps will increase your ability to connect with others.

Family: The talents of each child can differ and balancing praise accordingly can cause the atmosphere of the family culture to reveal what is important or not important (ex: sports or academics). The financial goals between spouses may be different. When the goals of each person in a household are acknowledged and given support, then the culture of the household will be healthier.

Community: What a non-profit views as a priority can differ from the people donating. The goals will have to be in line if they are going to be able to connect with the public.

Interacting appropriately:

Corporate: Business is no longer done with people who are "just like us." Hence, a middle manager must be aware of—and learn how to connect with—those who are different. Many middle managers—especially those who have been recently promoted—have no idea how to effectively function in their new roles. They often fly by the seat of their pants, trying to find their way as they go along.

Family: Conduct and actions are just as important today as they were 100 years ago. While we are around more people more often, understanding how to interact in multiple situations, including the ability to handle multiple activities, stresses, and expectations will be a necessary skill.

Community: This is big. How does one influence the culture of a community? I come from a place of non-judgment with my spirituality. Yet, others may have the same feeling but respect different rules of society. I like to call myself a republocrat. I am socially liberal but fiscally conservative. Don't roll your eyes; I am not going into politics. The choices I make and how I connect with my community are a reflection of my beliefs of how society should be run. I believe so many people want to judge others' actions but be judged by their own intentions. Have you ever said, "I can't believe they did that!" and in the same situation say with a soft voice, "I am sorry; my intentions were good." The culture of your community starts with you. Knowing your intentions, understanding others' actions, and leading when others won't are key skills in developing a positive community culture.

A class in leadership development can help crystallize objectives from day one, traverse the minefields you'll face on a daily basis, and avoid the pitfalls many executives experience once promoted to middle management. Employers in the 21st century are seeking employees who have advanced soft skills because they are more likely to: understand how to achieve results in a highly diverse workforce; identify and act on new ideas; be optimistic and open to change; and take an interest in and understand the overall structure of an organization (as opposed to just their own position).

Behind every long-term, successful leader is a team, family, or community. Becoming a comfortable leader means learning how to get—and keep—people that believe in you behind you. Great leaders aren't stagnant. Great parents change and grow. Communities evolve for better or worse.

So, the Connection Stage is all about being intentional with personal growth, understanding the purpose of others, and being clear on our own purpose.

My STRONG Blueprint™ can help you get started. It doesn't matter your education level, past mistakes, or lack of being clear on what you want from the future. Developing these three statements (purpose, passion, and vision) declare your belief in yourself. My experience, with executives to college students, has proven that, if you don't believe in something, you will fall for anything.

Here are my own personal purpose, passion, and vision statements:

My purpose statement: Through my enthusiasm, intuition, courage, and wisdom, I ignite a flame within others to do more, be more, and have more, so they can experience life to the fullest.

My passion statement: I love being inspirational and being a picture of hope. I enjoy igniting possibility thinking and helping others push their own boundaries as well as my own.

My vision statement: I see people around the world taking action, overcoming obstacles, and building confidence through my seminars, keynotes, and resources: *My Life Begins Next Monday…, Faith in 4D, My STRONG Blueprint, VisionQuest 2020, FaithQuest 2020,* and *Strong Success Academy for Leadership and Sales*.

Learn your purpose, passion, and vision. Create a family purpose, passion, and vision statement. Lead your community with purpose, passion, and vision. You can start with a free five-step guide on how and why to write a personal mission statement at www.MyLifeBeginsNextMonday.com. Enter code: STRONG.

The Connection Stage takes the most intentionality, the most learning, the most work. If you truly want to get to the next level of where you are at, in anything, it's all about your ability to connect with people.

And it starts with you.

THE APPLICATION BLUEPRINT

1. Write the top three feelings you love to feel:

1. _____
2. _____
3. _____

2. When do you find yourself lost in the moment?

_____
_____
_____

3. What communication skills do you need to develop?

1. _____
2. _____
3. _____

(Examples: Optimism, Empathy, Social Skills, Responsibility, Follow through, Encouragement, Leadership, Adapting to change.)

4. Describe how you manage the culture(s) you are a part of:

_____
_____
_____
_____

5. Write out your top three goals for the next year. Are they in line with your career and personal life, and how will they benefit the community?

_____
_____
_____
_____
_____
_____
_____
_____

6. Now, go to www.MyLifeBeginsNextMonday.com and download the Mission Statement worksheet and start your Strong Blueprint.

THE TAKEAWAY

What is one thing you can take away from this chapter and apply to your personal life?
_____
_____
_____

What is one thing you can take away from this chapter and apply to your business or career?
_____
_____
_____

What is one tangible, practical thing you can do today that will make a difference tomorrow?
_____
_____
_____

Connection

The blocks don't fit.
The blades of grass feel sharp as my feet press down.
The puzzle pieces are scattered.

Where do I start?

Persuaded by the prize.
The rewards so great, they distort our intentions.
Look how we justify.

Don't connect and we all lose.

Selfishness.
Self-centeredness.
Ulterior Motives.

Connect and Win.

Peace and gratefulness found.
Each soul exposed.
The significance is everlasting.

Chapter 7: Grace

The meaning of life.
The wasted years of life.
The poor choices of life.
God answers the mess of
life with one word: grace.

–Max Lucado

7

The temptation when you've made it this far is to think you've achieved perfection, that life will be easy from here on out. You haven't. It won't.

This is where Grace comes in. Grace is something we don't deserve.

Grace says, "It's okay that you've taken a step backward. Take a minute; then pick yourself up; dust yourself off; and get back in the game."

Grace says, "It's okay that you haven't conquered every fear, defeated every bad habit. No one is perfect. Keep trying."

You give yourself Grace first, so you can extend it to others. And, this might sound strange, but you've got to give God Grace too. He's going to let you down (not really, but it will seem like that when things aren't going your way), but you'll need to say, "I trust you, God. This isn't what I wanted, but I'm willing to stick with you and see what you've got planned."

God is there. He always was. We just don't always see it or feel it.

Be Kind to Yourself

Most of us are much more critical of ourselves than we realize. Over the years, I've been one of my own worst critics. Berating myself for getting into difficult situations, for poor judgment and bad decisions, for not making something of myself earlier than I did. Just like we talked about in previous chapters, a pessimistic, critical view of yourself will get you nowhere in life. Yes, we need to own our mistakes and accept our reality, but then we forgive ourselves and move past our past.

Criticizing yourself is a hard habit to break. Can you think of some negative self-talk that comes naturally to you? *You're not smart enough to do this job. Everyone else has her life together except you. You keep failing at the same thing over and over. You don't deserve to live your dreams.*

What are some kind, gentle, Grace-filled words you could say to yourself instead? The next time a negative thought comes along, parse the words and use gentler language. You'll find that, once you start doing this for yourself, you'll automatically apply this way of thinking to others as well.

Remember—we're to love others *as we love ourselves*. It's hard to truly love and connect with others—and offer them Grace—if we're not doing it with ourselves first.

When it comes to relationships, you have to be solid with who you are so that your Motivations are authentic. Love is a tricky thing. It's hard to find today. Everyone's looking in the wrong places, so to speak. Learn to love yourself first.

Positivity and kindness attract positivity and kindness. They just do. We don't get what we want; we get what we put out. So what you put out will definitely come back to you—usually many times over.

If you want more, it's not about *doing* more; it's about *being* more. You've got to forgive yourself, grant yourself a little Grace, and a little time to go out and do more, be more.

You want to think about all the things you like to do? Are you taking time to do that? Take 10 minutes every day. When was the last time you took a few minutes to ask yourself, "How could I create a different life?" (We'll come back to this in a bit.)

Making Things Right
Reconciliation is a big part of this Grace stage. Reconciling with yourself. Reconciling with others. Reconciling with God. Making things right all around.

Forgiveness is hard—especially if the other person hasn't expressed any remorse for what they did to you. Unfortunately, the bitterness we feel toward someone eats away at us far more than it bothers the other person. Letting go seems so hard but is one of the most freeing things we can do.

"Forgiveness is the key to action and freedom," Hannah Arendt says.

My Life Begins Next Monday...

"To forgive is to set a prisoner free and discover that the prisoner was you"

-Lewis B. Smedes

"To forgive is to set a prisoner free and discover that the prisoner was you," writes Lewis B. Smedes.

It is very rare that someone can move forward into their dream life while still holding on to old hurts and grievances. No matter how much happiness and fulfillment you find, that bitterness will creep in and try to lessen it, even ruin it. This book would never have happened if I hadn't finally forgiven my mother, myself, and those who hurt or used me.

"Forgiveness is about empowering yourself, rather than empowering your past," says author and preacher, T.D. Jakes.

Forgiveness is key. Even if the person doesn't deserve it. This is about *you* and the freedom you'll find when you forgive. Can you think of someone (or a few people) you need to forgive before you move forward?

Kristin's Story
As we explore grace and forgiveness, I want to share a powerful story with you (with permission from my friend, Kristin). Kristin's teenage years were all about hanging around with the wrong crowd, searching for acceptance. The kids around her were drinking and doing drugs, so Kristin did too. She started off "easy" with alcohol and pot.

She was pregnant by age 16. They got married and then separated a year later when he came out of the closet as gay. She was 17 with a child (a son named Haden) and knew nothing about being a mother.

Little by little, she moved up the drug world ladder. She was 21 when she first tried cocaine. "Cocaine helped me drink more and keep up with everyone," she says. "Of course, it ends up controlling your life."

While the high lasted, she felt on top of the world, happy, in control. "The whole time I was trying to fill a void inside of me," she says. "I didn't know what I wanted, but I was never happy, never satisfied with anything in my life."

She would get arrested for little things from time to time and end up on probation, but it was never enough to scare her, to make her realize she could lose something.

It wasn't long before she was pregnant again. She went back and forth about getting an abortion and actually made the appointment. When the day came, she couldn't go through with it. She doesn't know if it was God or her conscience but something told her, "He didn't ask for this. He's going to be amazing."

Josh was born a few months later. Kristin had continued to use drugs throughout her entire pregnancy up until the night before he was born. She was living in Texas on her own (Haden was living with his paternal grandmother.). To this day, she's not sure how she avoided the state stepping in on Josh's behalf.

She was honest with her doctor about her drug use and promised to go to 30-day rehab after he was born. She did well (and even got to take Josh with her), but 30 days isn't really long enough to get clean and change your whole thinking pattern. As soon as she got out, she went right back to drugs.

A change in environment is also key when you're trying to quit. Kristin moved right back to the same area with the same friends. When Josh was six months old, she revoked her probation, drove without a license, and ended up in jail for a month. Her mom came to get Josh.

When she got out of jail, she was still on Texas state probation. That's when she met the father of her next baby. He used needles, and after a month together, Kristin was using them as well.

"That completely took over my life," she said. "It just took me over the edge."

Her boyfriend was so happy she'd done it, and all she remembers is wanting to stop the pain. Wanting to forget about everything she'd lost, especially her sons. She played the victim and blamed everyone else for her problems.

For six months, they sold meth to make a living and support their drug habit. Then they got caught. By the time the verdict came out (a federal indictment), Kristin was three months pregnant and in jail for another probation violation. Her mom was by her side when her sentence was handed down. Ten years to life. They told her she was looking at about 17 years. Her mom's pain over the verdict was almost too much for Kristin to take, but her time in prison turned out to be a blessing.

"It's probably the best thing that ever happened to me," she says. "I couldn't do drugs, and it brought me closer to God and changed my whole direction in life."

No one would ever guess, by talking to Kristin today, that she is a former drug addict who has spent time in prison. She is well-rounded, stable, well-spoken, and passionate.

What was her lowest point while in jail? "When I had Jonathan," she says, "they did a c-section and gave me anesthesia. I didn't know anyone. My greatest fear was that they would switch my baby with someone else's while I was knocked out."

Kristin remains ever grateful for the family support she had while in prison. Some of the women who had babies in jail never got to see them again. Some had life sentences. Some had no one to come get their kids. Josh went to live with her mom.

She ended up serving almost five years in a federal prison. She spent her time productively—figuring out what she wanted in life and how to stay out of jail. She successfully completed a nine-month residential drug rehab program and calls it a godsend.

The next year she started changing other behaviors little by little. "I cussed like a sailor before and don't cuss at all now. God took it away." She got saved and baptized. She was a new person.

But that doesn't mean life is easy.

Because of all she's been through, Kristin has so much to say about grace and forgiveness. Over time, while in prison, she was able to forgive herself for everything she had done, everyone she had hurt—especially her boys.

"Who am I to not forgive myself when God forgives me?" she says.

It was hard though. Someone else was raising her children. They lived in three separate homes (Jonathan was with his dad's sister).

Whenever she feels the guilt creep in, she reminds herself that it's not what God wants, and it's not what her kids need.

The hardest person to forgive? Her mom. Kristin admits she was very rebellious toward her mom when she was on drugs. When she got locked up, at least six months passed before she called her mother. Her mom was so thankful to hear she was alive, and they started rebuilding their relationship. But she also dropped a bomb.

Her mom was in the process of adopting Josh. Kristin was angry at first. How dare she? But then she realized it was for the best. They had no idea how long Josh would live with her mom. It was best that he belong to her legally. Kristin knew it was her own choices that made this necessary.

When she got out of jail, the realization that Josh belonged to her parents hit hard. "I thought I had worked through everything," she says. "I had written her a really long letter. The program I did was based on my needs. You go in there and talk to your counselor, and they set you up with a treatment plan. You read books, write reports and letters, go through stages to get emotions out, work on coping skills for when you get out. How are you going to react? I thought I had gotten completely over it. But when I got home, it hit me that he was theirs. She raises him differently than I feel I would. That's a big thing."

Kristin struggled with what felt like her mom's betrayal for a long time. "It still rears its ugly head every once in a while if I'm not careful," she says. "I just have to put myself in her shoes. She had no idea I was going to get out, turn my life around, and live out every dream she's ever wanted for me. How could she have?"

What advice does Kristin have for others who are struggling with forgiveness? "When you hold on to bitterness against someone, their lives go on," she says, "and you're left there holding on to the anger and bitterness. You're not hurting them in any way. You're only hurting yourself. It doesn't get you anywhere. No one wants to be around you."

What are some things that helped her let go of that bitterness and anger? "Growing my relationship with God. Reading the Bible. Taking classes and Bible studies. God would talk to me through his Word. Writing letters was also healing. I got all my feelings out without worrying about judgment or about what the other person would say."

What a powerful story. Thank you, Kristin, for so bravely sharing your story of forgiveness and grace.

"No" Is Not a Four-Letter Word
Grace is also about saying "no," believe it or not. You've got to give yourself the grace to say no. This is so hard for so many of us. Women, in particular, are more apt to take on much more than they can handle. In part, it's because we're taught from an early age to be pleasers. Trying to please can lead to fatigue, burnout, stress, and unnecessary illness.

Learning to say no is one of the most powerful actions you can take as a human being, especially when you decide to pursue your passion. It's not about being rude, nasty, or selfish; it's actually a gift of love—one you give yourself.

Saying no allows you to be a healthier, happier, more fulfilled you. This "you" is a better person to everyone in your life, e.g., your partner, children, family, friends, boss, etc.

Yes, you might be qualified to do each and every thing that's asked of you, but that doesn't mean you have to do it. And think of it this way: every time you say no, you're providing someone else with an opportunity to serve, shine, and be a blessing.

Trade Your Worry for Wonder
Along these lines, friend, can I give you one of the most important pieces of advice you'll ever hear?

Stop worrying.

I mean it. Stop right now. No more worrying. Don't do it. Don't give in to it. No matter what's going on in your life, how much stress you're under, decide right now that you aren't going to worry.

Your life does not begin next Monday…it starts today!

Your life does not begin next Monday...it starts today!

When I catch myself worrying today, I make it a goal to think about the moment I am in, in that moment. Seriously. This last year of my life, I have had a really sweet relationship with the Lord. I've decided to take his words to heart, to trust him, and to give up my worrying.

I've replaced it with something much better: *wonder*.

When you wonder what's going to happen next instead of worrying what's going to happen, your life will change. When you're confident you can make it through whatever comes your way, it creates a calm in your life, a peace worth more than anything money can buy.

You may be thinking, "That sounds great, Shari, but how do I go from worry to wonder?"

I believe it starts with the belief that there are no mistakes. You heard me right. There are NO mistakes. Everything has a purpose. Even getting cut off in traffic. It's all part of a divine plan. It may be a part of someone else's bigger plan, and you were able to handle the distraction, so that's why you found yourself in their path.

When we choose to live with the core belief that there is a plan, even if we don't know what it is, it brings peace to our heart and frees our mind to focus on solutions and possibilities. This will lead to a fulfilled life.

The sun is an exact distance from the earth so we don't freeze or burn up. The wind blows to carry good weather in and bad weather out. Everything has a purpose. Including you.

Let me ask you a rhetorical question. You're still here, aren't you? Is that a yes? You're still here? After all you've been through, you're still here.

So, why do you worry? It's a waste of your precious time. Worrying only causes more problems, more stress, more physical duress. The Bible says, "Who, by worrying, can add a day to his life?" It's true. Where did we get the idea that worrying helps anything or changes anything? All it does is make things worse.

Let's get rid of worry once and for all. And let's trade it in for wonder.

Replacing Bad Habits with Awesome Ones
Another big obstacle to achieving our dreams? Bad habits. Some of them we acquired while we were in the Survival Stage, some we've struggled with our whole lives.

It's time for them to go.

Some will be easier to shed than others. Some will take all the determination and willpower you've got. But, if you're serious about moving forward and pursuing your dream life, there is no room for bad habits of any kind.

There are methods, if you will, for controlling your own habits, and it starts there. You persevere through something, and you have to learn to control your thoughts and actions. It's a system. Systems are solutions.

I teach from the Pat Summit approach. If you're unfamiliar with Pat, she's the world-class former coach of the University of Tennessee's women's basketball team. She would take her team in at halftime and ask, "What are the three things we need to improve on?"

I teach this every day to entrepreneurs. What are three things I did well today, and what are three things I need to improve upon? Not, what did I do badly, but what do I need to improve upon? There's a difference.

You can do this yourself (or with a coach) every day, week, month. You need to be willing to ask yourself these questions. Don't justify the answer. Just ask the question and answer honestly. It's awesome. You'll see. This method will help you get rid of bad habits that are creeping in and getting in the way of your dreams.

First, you need to recognize bad habits for what they are and make the connection that they're getting in the way of your goals.

Here's a personal example. I have a habit of eating junk food at night. I eat pretty healthy during the day, but if there's junk food in the house, I have a hard time resisting it in the evenings.

Another bad habit I have: sitting at my desk for 12 hours straight—especially if I'm on a roll. You know how it is. The creative juices get flowing, and who wants to interrupt that? But it's not good for me mentally (or physically) to sit in one place and work for so long. I'm just asking for burnout.

Bad habits need to be replaced by good habits, or you just find yourself back in the same cycle again. For example, to combat my bad habit of sitting at my desk for 12 hours, I've built in time during the day—on my calendar—to take breaks. Just like I would stop my work for an appointment or a speaking engagement, I stop what I'm doing when it's break time.

What bad habits are you hanging onto? And what good habits will you replace those bad habits with?

Managing Your Time to Your Advantage
All of us, if we're honest, struggle with managing our time. We might not realize it, but we're pretty good at wasting time without even noticing. I encourage you to take one day and record everything you do in 15-minute increments.

I was taught this method by another coach. It is called the 15-Minute Miracle. This method will give you insight into two things: where you're wasting time and where your priorities are—even if you say they're something different. The 15-Minute Miracle will not only help you control your time; it will help you figure out who you are.

Some of us need to learn self-control. Controlling our thoughts and habits is a big challenge, but it's the only way to get to do what we want to do. We can't blame our circumstances or other people for where we are in life. And you can't blame it on the environment, our friends, or Obama Care.

Everyone got right where they are because of the choices they made, and everyone's going to get to where they're going because of the choices they make. (That's the good news *and* the bad news.)

So, what are some ways to put more time into your day? Go to bed earlier. Just 30 minutes earlier. I love getting up. Some people say, "I'm a night owl." And that is fine, as long as you're doing something productive. You'll get more done before 8:00 in the morning than you will in the evening. The night should be used for reflection, not work.

When you go to bed earlier, you'll also have more strength to get through the next day. When you get up in the morning, have a schedule of what you need to do. Get things out of the way. If you have a load of laundry to do, do it first, so you're not thinking about it.

Plan an hour in the morning to get stuff done around the house.

Plan an hour for your work plan, to plan out what you're going to do through the day. Try to get 5-10 things done in a day. Not too few and not too many.

Do not get sidetracked. It's so easy to get off course. The 15-minute miracle will show you how many small increments of time you're wasting throughout the day. Randomly surfing the Internet, watching soap operas, flipping through channels. What are your biggest time-wasters? (These will show up as you chart your day.)

One last important piece of advice: don't get frustrated. When you get frustrated, that leads to being overwhelmed, and then we end up stuck.

Life is all about energy. Every one of us has 100% to give. Not 120%, not 80%. 100%. Where are you using your 100%?

Redirect Your Life in 30 Minutes
The STRONG 15-Minute Miracle to Taking Back Your Time is a great tool for figuring out how you've been spending your time, but you'll also need a personal development plan to help you map out where you want to go in life.

Ever heard of speed dating? It's an event where you meet a few people in a short amount of time, spend a few minutes talking to each person, then decide if you'd like to spend more time with any of those you've met. A highly effective personal development plan can be done in the same manner—and it can change your entire life.

When many think of personal development plans, they tend to overthink it, spending time pondering personal growth goals, reading self-improvement ebooks, and perhaps even researching personal and professional development seminars and gurus.

This is much like dating without knowing what you want.

Or, as I like to call it (as I see it), stalling.

One of the quickest ways to stop stalling and start achieving your personal development goals is to act—now. Much like speed dating, you sit down, mentally "interview" yourself to clarify what you want, then follow up and make it happen.

To this end, here are five steps to creating a personal development plan—one that could literally change your life—in 30 minutes or less.

1. Your Ideal Life: Write down your ideal life; i.e., what your life would look like if money, family, health, etc., were not hindering factors.

Purpose: To crystallize what utopia would look like for you.

2. Segment and Grade Your Life: Write down the main areas of your life and grade them on a scale of 1 to 10, with 1 being very unhappy and 10 being extremely happy.

Purpose: To see in black and white where you're most/least happy so you can jump start the self-improvement process. For example, your list might look like this:

Career: 4
Personal Relationships: 6
Health: 5
Family: 7

3. Create a "Today" Action Plan: What can you start doing today to start seeing results?

Purpose: To stop stalling and start acting on your personal growth goals—immediately. For example, if you're 20 pounds overweight, you could start with the health category and commit to walking/exercising at least 30 minutes a day.

4. Create a Weekly Action Plan: Every week, carve out an hour to work on future goals.

Purpose: To tackle goals you can't achieve immediately. For example, if you desperately want to change jobs, devote an hour each week to doing something toward finding/training for a new position. It could be anything from updating your resume to attending a Chamber of Commerce meeting and networking.

5. Assess Goals Weekly: A personal development plan is not a noun, e.g., a thing. It's a verb; a living, breathing document that must be acted upon regularly. Hence, it should be assessed regularly—at least on a weekly basis.

Purpose: To stay on track with all goals.

What do you think? Is this five-step plan something you can do? As a success coach, I help people all the time with planning their lives (including the 4 D's—decide it, define it, design it, do it), and our success rate is just about 100%.

More on Attitude Opportunity
During the time of my divorce and car accident, I lost everything. It was more than just money and stuff. But because I had moved from Survival and Denial to Acceptance and Motivation, I was able to see this horrific experience as an "Attitude Opportunity."

Here's the thing. There isn't any real secret to maintaining a positive attitude. It's a choice. Attitude is a frame of mind. It affects how we see everything, approach everything, and experience everything. Remember Forrest Gump's mom? As she was dying, she told her son, "Forrest, life is like a box of chocolates; you never know what you are going to get."

She was giving Forrest the gift of perspective. We can't control everything that happens to us, but we can control how we react and choose to see the positive. That's what I call an attitude opportunity.

In 2009, I was managing a group from North Carolina to Portland, Maine for an online media company (mentioned in Chapter 4). During that year, the recession was hitting the automobile industry significantly, and we worked specifically with auto dealers. We were negative $76k in revenue for the year through August. We had more dealers go out of business than any other region in the U.S.

This was a tough, tough job, and my sales team wasn't feeling it. But each one of them decided to view these dire circumstances as an attitude opportunity. They could have run for the hills, or at least switched jobs, but they didn't. They came up with a solution, changed their perspective, and in the next three months, with no special sales incentive, just a change of attitude, sold around $86k. They overcame the negative.

It was an attitude opportunity.

A friend of mine is an avid golfer. Every time she lands in a bunker, she says, "Yes!" She gets out of the sand 9 out of 10 times. She makes it an attitude opportunity.

Every moment is a new opportunity to choose your attitude. Making the right choice can change your life.

I was blessed with an invitation to join a group of women for three days every year, at the beginning of June. There are no expectations of each other; it is all about relaxing, swimming, and enjoying each other's friendships. The FPW group accepted me and taught me in our first meeting what attitude opportunity really means: live in the moment and have no regrets.

What I Want For You
My hope for this book is to inspire you, to help you see yourself in my story. To raise your awareness of yourself and your circumstances, to help you forgive yourself for your past mistakes, to convince you to grant yourself grace, to help you see the good in yourself, and to inspire you to share YOU with more people who need what you have to offer.

And you do have something to offer. We all do.

THE APPLICATION BLUEPRINT

1. Write down some negative self-talk you have used in the past/are currently using.
___
___
___
___
___

2. Now, replace each of those negative phrases with a kinder, gentler, grace-filled truth.
___
___
___
___
___

3. In what ways do you need to forgive yourself?
___
___
___
___
___

4. Who are some people you need to forgive in order to move forward with the life you want and deserve?

In what ways do you believe forgiving your past will empower your future?

_____
_____
_____
_____
_____

5. In what areas of your life do you need to begin saying "no"?

_____
_____
_____
_____
_____

6. What bad habits need to go, and what good habits will you implement to replace them?

_____
_____
_____
_____
_____

7. What are some of your biggest worries (fears), and how might you turn them into wonder?

_____
_____
_____
_____
_____

THE TAKEAWAY

What is one thing you can take away from this chapter and apply to your personal life?
_____
_____
_____

What is one thing you can take away from this chapter and apply to your business or career?
_____
_____
_____

What is one tangible, practical thing you can do today that will make a difference tomorrow?
_____
_____
_____

YOU

You are amazing.
You are gentle.
You are soulful.
Thank you for being you.

You are empathetic.
You are a ray of sunshine.
You are dew in the morning.
Thank you for being you.

You are in the moment.
You were there then.
You will be there tomorrow.
Thank you for being you.

You are a gift.
You are a bow.
You are so valuable.
Thank you for being you.

It starts with you.
It will end with you.
You are you.
Thank you for being you.

The Final Word

Friend, there is no reason on earth to settle for less than all you've ever envisioned, hoped for, and dreamed of in life. The key to a better life is to have goals and dreams and a plan to achieve them.

Set that bar high. Dream big. Go for the impossible. Don't just do what you're good at. Find the space where your strengths and talents meet your greatest passion. Do not let life pass you by. We all want more. We all want to do more, be more.

People who are serious about their dreams find a way to make them happen. They don't let anything stand in their way. Not fear, not insecurity, not lack of any kind.

Make your life count. Figure out what it is you can do better than anyone else, that will make you stand out. Be significant.

As my mentor John Maxwell says, "Once you get a taste of significance, you're never going to settle for success again."

Take control of your life and do not be afraid of the journey. Embrace the wonderment. Others will notice and appreciate the difference in you. You'll inspire them to live bigger lives too.

There's nothing in life that should hold you back from living. Don't be afraid to do something because you're afraid you can't. You have the power to make your own choices. You have the power to live the life you want to live.

It's going to pass by you quickly. I think it was Eleanor Roosevelt who said, "Life is like a parachute jump. You've got to get it right the first time." Sure, you get second chances, but you only have one life.

You were made to live an abundant life, a full life, a satisfying and significant life. You were made for a purpose, to reach for the sky, to live your wildest dreams.

Now, go do it.
And friend,
Thank you for being you.

Shari

Learn More about My Strong Blueprint Manual and other resources at
www.MyLifeBeginsNextMonday.book

Learn More about Joining the Strong Success Academy and the Passport Club
www.StrongSuccessAcademy.com

Receive a chapter of
Success in 4D:
The Simple Formula for Achieving Your Goals

And

Faith In 4D:
God's Simple Plan For Your Life

www.StrongFreeBook.com

Shari Strong

Take the Energy Leadership Assessment for ½ price. (code: book)

www.StrongSuccessAcademy.com/Assessment

Become a Certified Life Coach
www.Ipec.com

Special Acknowledgments:

My Butterfly Purpose Friends: Bridgett McAdams, Kim Borrelli, and Deb Ingino

God is so good! He used you so perfectly and in his perfect time. Always have the peace knowing that God is working through you.

Thank you to the pastors and ministers God put in my path during the past three years of writing this. May you be at peace that God used you to influence me in the most amazing way:

John Maxwell, Justin P., Jan R., Kary O., Dan C., George P., Steve D., Stephen P., Rick K., Brett T., Larry S., Roger H., Randy S., Victor A.

Marla Taviano:

You have been patient, flexible, amazing, and a great partner. Without you, this would not have come to fruition. Thank you for being you!

John Maxwell Team:

This journey has been amazing! And I am so thankful for each of you! Thank you for your support, your guidance, your partnerships, love, and prayers.

IPEC Team, Bruce Schneider, and Luke Iorio:

Enrolling with IPEC was the first true investment in myself and everything changed in my life after that first module. I was broken, and you helped me become whole again. Thank you does not seem enough. But…THANK YOU! A special thank you to Barb Heenan, Raechel Anderson Dressler, Laura Fischer, and "My Graduating Class." You allowed me space to be humbled, grow, cry, and laugh.

Former Colleagues at Cars.com:

I cannot express how much my time at cars.com meant to me. You allowed space to grow, helped build my confidence, and it was ultimately where I really got to develop my love of leading people. I learned from you, and my hope is that you all reach your dreams.

CPSIA information can be obtained
at www.ICGtesting.com
Printed in the USA
LVOW09s1919020417
529363LV00001B/1/P